DISCOVER LONDON DOCKLANDS

A to Z Illustrated Souvenir Guide

Professor S K Al Naib

A Great Opening For the Docks

In 1802 the West India Docks (side picture) were opened with a flourish. The following is from a report that appeared in *The Times* on 27 August 1802, giving an account of the event.

"These docks were, on Monday last, filled with water by means of apertures made for that purpose, and yesterday was the day fixed upon for the grand ceremony of receiving the first ship into the great dock.

"About 12 o'clock, the outer gates communicating between the river and the entrance basin were opened, and the ship was towed in by men on each side of the basin, who were about one hundred in number.

"The motion of the ship through the basin was very slow. At 1 o'clock, she entered the great dock; immediately on which the company on board of her, together with all the people assembled along the shore, gave three cheers. The band of music on board, as well as the band of the West London Militia, which was on shore, played *God Save The Queen.*

"The vessel was then fastened to one of the moorings that lay next to the entrance basin, of which there are twenty four in the dock.

"The dock itself, appearing like a great lake, was an object of beauty and astonishment.

"The warehouses(top picture), are the grandest the most commodious and spacious we have ever seen, and are capable of containing a vast quantity of goods."

Today, only two of these magnificent warehouses survive in the shadow of the new Canary Wharf Complex awaiting renovation.

Guide to the Book

This is the third of the illustrated guide books on London Docklands written specially for Londoners, tourists and sightseers who wish to explore the old and new Docklands through walks and use of the Docklands Light Railway or buses. The book takes you through parts of this district's glorious history and its dramatic regeneration over the past ten years. It contains many pictures, illustrations and maps to help you with your reading or visit. It is equally a panoramic guide to Docklands from the River Thames. The magnificent restored historic buildings and the new developments, as seen from a river boat, are described under each area of Docklands. London Docklands comprise four major areas, namely Wapping and Limehouse; Isle of Dogs with its Enterprise Zone; the South Bank and Surrey Docks; and the Royal Docks. Tower Bridge represents "The Gateway" at the western end of the district.

In this book a description of the major new developments, conversions of historic warehouses, conservation schemes and heritage trails in each of these areas is accompanied by detailed area and location maps with reference numbers to developments which you may like to consult. Each page concentrates on one or two major schemes and surrounding developments. Subsidiary maps are provided for heritage trails and where a high concentration of sites of interest are located in a small area.

The feature number in parenthesis at the end of entries is the reference number of the insertion on the location map for the area. The maps are shown on the following pages:

Travelling to Docklands couldn't be easier - rail, road and river transport maps are shown on the insides of the front and back covers. By rail, the Docklands Light Railway provides access to most areas from Bank Station; the East London Line goes south to Surrey Docks. By road, connections are easy to the A13, A406, M11 and M25; for driving south there are Blackwall and Rotherhithe tunnels. By river, a riverbus service extends from Charing Cross to Greenwich and beyond. By air, London City Airport links the capital with UK and European cities. By buses, there are numerous routes serving Docklands through the City to the West End.

Visitors' guides at a glance for excursions, river trips and day drives are provided:

I hope you enjoy reading the book, benefit and relax from a tour of these historic Docklands.

Seventh Edition

The first printing of 2500 copies was sold out within two and a half months of publication in June 1992, and it has now been reprinted for the seventh time to meet continuing demad. Sincere thanks are due to the public for their generous support.

ISBN 1 8745 36 007

First Printing June 1992, Second Printing October 1992, Third Printing March 1993, Fourth Edition March 1994, Fifth Edition March 1995, Sixth Edition October 1996, Seventh Edition July 1998.

Internationally Acknowledged Books by the Author

"Fluid Mechanics, Hydraulics and Envir. Eng"	ISBN 1 8745 36 066
"Applied Hydraulics, Hydrology and Envir. Eng"	ISBN 1 8745 36 058
"Jet Mechanics and Hydraulic Structures"	ISBN 0 9019 87 832
"Experimental Fluid Mech. and Hyd. Modelling"	ISBN 1 8745 36 090
"London Dockland Guide" Heritage Panorama	ISBN 1 8745 36 031
"London Illustrated" History, Current & Future	ISBN 1 8745 36 015
"Discover London Docklands" A to Z Guide	ISBN 1 8745 36 007
"London Docklands" Past, Present and Future	ISBN 1 8745 36 023
"European Docklands" Past, Present and Future	ISBN 0 9019 87 824
"Dockland" Historical Survey	ISBN 0 9089 87 800

The author is Professor of Civil Engineering and Head of Department at the University of East London, England.
(Tel: 0181 590 7000/7722 ext 2478/2531,   Fax: 0181 849 3423)

Please Order through: Research Books, P. O. Box 82, Romford, Essex RM6 5BY, Great Britain.

Printed by Ashmead Press, London.

Preface

Written for Londoners, tourists and sightseers, this book is a comprehensive illustrated guide to London Docklands. All the major new developments and historic sights of conservation areas from Tower Bridge in the west to the Royal Docks in the east are described. Like other tourists attractions, Docklands yields its secrets to the visitor who is patient to discover what the local East Enders know. To help you on your way, the book is devised so that each page describes a place of interest. You can pick up at any point, leave parts or enjoy a riverbus excursion along the Thames.

The book serves as a unique reference for business people, the general public, local and government departments, private and commercial developers and other organisations. It is useful for use in schools and colleges in the teaching of architecture, engineering, geography, planning, design and technology, history and art. Sections describe the numerous conservation areas with their historic buildings which have shaped the district's environmental heritage. The successful maintenance of this heritage is of fundamental importance to all those who live, work or visit the dynamic environment.

The spectacular renaissance of Docklands is now well advanced with magnificently restored warehouses and modern new buildings preserving, and contributing to, the character of the historic area and providing new homes and offices. The Docklands Light Railway and the London City Airport are tangible development assets, and exciting new leisure facilities are flourishing along the extensive waterfront.

Today, London Docklands is one of the most exciting commercial and residential development districts in the world. It has become one of London's business centres with its own bustling community and unique waterside environment. The past few years have seen new life breathed into the long dormant areas of London Docklands. It is not merely a physical transformation which has taken place, but a change in the urban environment and way of life. The historic Docklands is one of the most fascinating areas of London. It is a place of rich tradition and great contrasts. Since 1981, the 22 square kilometres of Docklands has undergone a remarkable rebuilding. Thousands of new homes have been built, many new companies have moved in, and huge commercial floor space has been created.

London Docklands is an outstanding urban redevelopment programme in Europe, besides its unique location near the old City of London. Public transport facilities to and from London Docklands are being extended. London City Airport has scheduled flights to major UK and European Cities. The Docklands Light Railway has proved a major success. The Riverbus functions on the broadest highway in London!

The regeneration of Docklands has been stimulated by international developers from North America, Europe, the Middle East, Australia and Hong Kong. In terms of investment, they recognised the prime locations and cost benefits of Docklands vast areas and were prepared to take the risk and long term view. Regeneration is about people and their work and whilst investment and buildings provide the operating framework, it is essential to create the right environment. Docklands have undoubtly provided a splendid waterscape environment and have enabled invaluable experience in urban renewal nationally and internationally.

From London Bridge along the river waterfront to the Royal Docks, £9 billion have been invested into exciting new office complexes, beautiful homes and many other attractions, giving Docklands in East London a dramatic regeneration into one of the most attractive water cities of the world. Architecturally, the restoration integrates with its environment by responding to the historical forms and materials found in the area, while an infusion of modern design attempts to create a development of nautical relevance.

Docklands is divided into four separate areas; Wapping and Limehouse, the Isle of Dogs, Royal Docks, Surrey Docks including South Bank the area to the West of Tower Bridge on the southside of the River Thames. The Isle of Dogs has become a mainly office location and Canary Wharf alone accounts for nearly one million square metres of office space. The new international financial centre of Canary Wharf with its beautiful environment surrounded by office and retail complexes, including nearby Harbour Exchange and South Quay Plaza, is dominating the city skyline. Already more than a billion pounds has been spent in renovating historic warehouses, including the Anchor Brewhouse and Butlers Wharf next to the Tower Bridge. The revitalized part of the South Bank called London Bridge City is a most impressive urban renewal of its kind.

Life in Docklands is not all buildings; there are plenty of leisure activities and shopping facilities. Docklands has many riverside public houses steeped in history including the Prospect of Whitby (said to be the oldest in London), the Town of Ramsgate, The Grapes, The Angel, The Mayflower and many others. Sport is well catered for including the London Arena and the watersport centres of Millwall, Shadwell Basin and Greenland Dock; the Yacht Haven at St. Katharine Docks and the South Dock Marina are the Cannes of Docklands. Beckton has a dry-ski slope and an impressive indoor cricket and bowls pavilion. Docklands boasts a fine selection of wine bars and restaurants offering "Eastenders" food and international cuisine. Museums house diverse subjects such as the activities in old docklands, naval history and modern design. There are exciting shopping precincts including the historic Tobacco Dock and the Surrey Quays. There is much landscaping to admire, new tree-lined squares and gardens to wander through and picturesque riverside walkways in which to relax and enjoy.

The tourist centre of Docklands is St. Katharine Docks Conservation Area, site of London World Trade Centre and Commodity Quay, the home of the London Commodity Exchange. The beautiful marina, with its historic boats, individual shops and entertainment in Ivory House and Tower Hotel, has become a popular rendezvous for Londoners and foreign visitors all year round.

LONDON DOCKLANDS

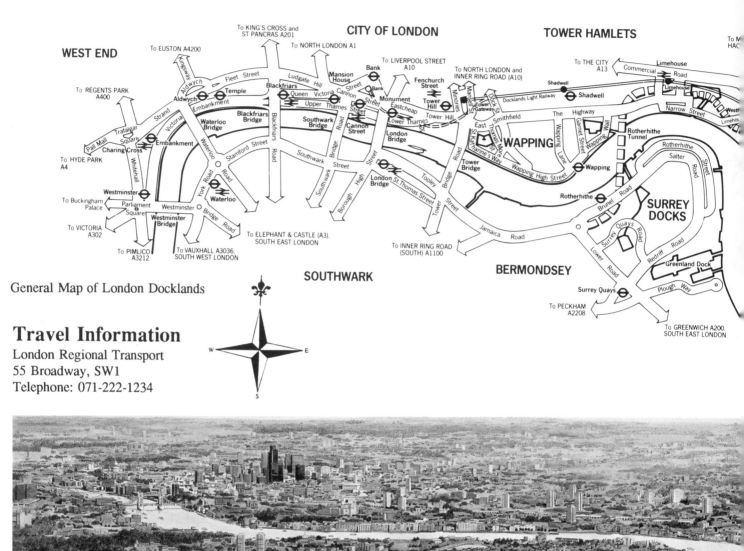

General Map of London Docklands

Travel Information

London Regional Transport
55 Broadway, SW1
Telephone: 071-222-1234

London Docklands from Greenwich

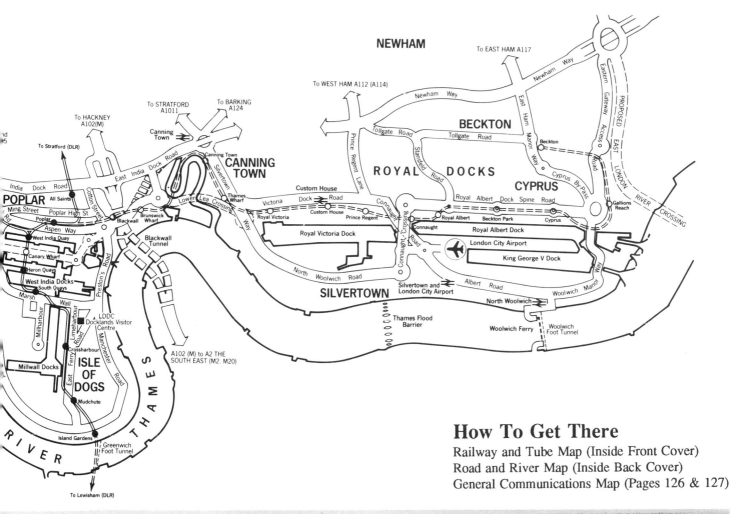

How To Get There

Railway and Tube Map (Inside Front Cover)
Road and River Map (Inside Back Cover)
General Communications Map (Pages 126 & 127)

CONTENTS

TOURIST INFORMATION CENTRES

Tower of London
Tower Hill, EC3.
Telephone: 071-730 3488

Docklands Light Railway
Tower Gate Station, E1.
Telephone 071-474-5555

Docklands Visitor Centre
3 Millharbour, E14.
Telephone: 071-512-3000

Canary Wharf Visitor Centre
1 Canada Square, E14.
Telephone: 071-510-3051

LONDON DOCKLANDS TOURIST ATTRACTIONS

INTERESTING PLACES TO VISIT

Docklands, only a short journey from Bank Station, is one of the most exciting new tourist attractions in London. A wealth of beautiful historic warehouses, old riverside pubs and impressive new developments enchant the wandering visitor. Whether you intend to find out about the glorious history of the area, or whether you are fascinated by the sheer scale of new developments such as the Canary Wharf, Docklands is a place of discovery. A quick glance at the list below will reveal some of the many places of interest. On the page indicated below you will find information and a map reference to these and other attractions. Enjoy your visit!

TOURIST INFORMATION CENTRE
London Tourist Board
26 Grosvenor Gardens, SW1
Telephone 071-730-3488

LONDON DOCKLANDS RIVERSIDE VIEWS

RIVERBUS TOURS TO ENJOY

London is one of the most beautiful cities in the world. Whether for business or pleasure, a trip down the River Thames is a delightful experience. Starting from the majestic Houses of Parliament down river to the Royal Observatory at Greenwich, the restored historical buildings and the exciting new developments pass by to show London at its best. Details of the riverbus tours from Charing Cross Pier to Docklands are given on page 133. Views are listed below in the order in which they would be seen travelling down river. With the exception of London Bridge City on the South Bank, all views are east of Tower Bridge. The page numbers refer to the features in the book.

WAPPING AND LIMEHOUSE

ISLE OF DOGS

ROYAL DOCKS

SURREY DOCKS

Riverbus

The Riverbus runs a regular service between Charing Cross Pier and Greenwich Pier which calls at London Bridge City Pier and West India Pier. Fast hourly service to London City Airport is also available.

Telephone 071-512-0555.

LONDON DOCKLANDS HERITAGE TRAILS

CONSERVATION AREAS TO SEE

Docklands is one of London's oldest Thamesside settlements, rich in maritime legend and tradition - a heritage that has made Docklands one of the most famous areas in the world. Many of the historic sites and features of architectural interest are located in Conservation Areas in the unique riverside parishes of Wapping, Limehouse, Isle of Dogs, Bermondsey and Rotherhithe - providing a perfect setting for these beautiful waterscape areas and the dramatic new developments emerging alongside the restored warehouses. Most of these historic buildings have been listed by the Secretary of State for the Environment. The eighteen designated conservation areas are given below with page numbers for information and maps to help you with your tours. Visitors are always welcome.

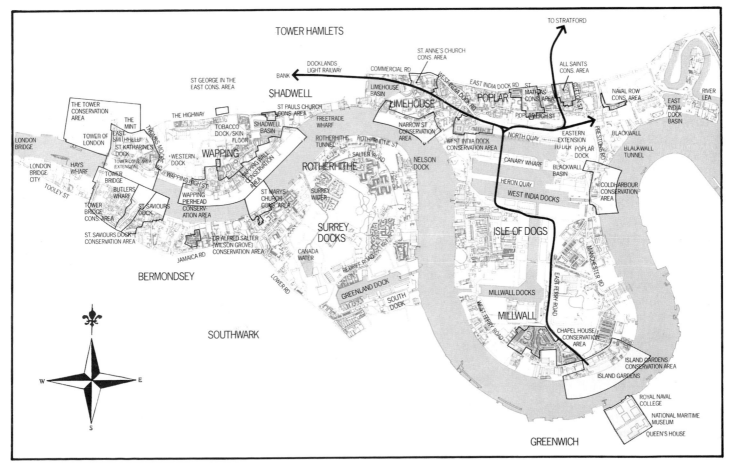

Map of Docklands Conservation Areas

LONDON DOCKLANDS

WAPPING AND LIMEHOUSE

Wapping

This area covers a strip of Docklands stretching between the Tower of London and Limehouse. It is the most ancient of the various riverside parishes outside the City of London. Its long riverfront on the north bank of the Thames, old streets and small basins together with a large stock of historic warehouses have proved considerable attractions for commercial and residential developments. Over the past two decades, the area has been transformed into a fashionable residential area for the city merchants and business people.

The early developments included the World Trade Centre in St. Katharine Docks, which provides a focal base for international companies. Major developments recently completed include the Tobacco Dock, which is the most exciting retail development in Docklands to date. Numerous conversions and new buildings have taken place along the river frontage. News International built their printing works at London Docks site.

Wapping is now well developed and established as a highly desirable district of London, being within easy distance of the city. The population of Wapping and Limehouse is around 13,000 in 1991, over double the figure of 1981. The main outstanding projects are the reclamation of the Limehouse Basin. Construction of the Limehouse and Poplar Link Roads is due for completion in 1993.

Limehouse

Limehouse, which lies between Wapping and the Isle of Dogs, has attracted a number of well known personalities. The oldest part of the area is Narrow Street with some of its houses dating back to the early 18th century. Angie from Eastenders, Dr. Owen the former SDP leader and the late Sir David Lean the film director, made their homes in Limehouse. Limehouse has a number of riverside schemes, such as Keepier Wharf, Blyth's Wharf and Duke Shore Wharf. Workers in the high technology area of the Isle of Dogs have developed a taste for living in the quaint historic environment of Wapping and Limehouse.

St. Paul's Church
Conservation Area

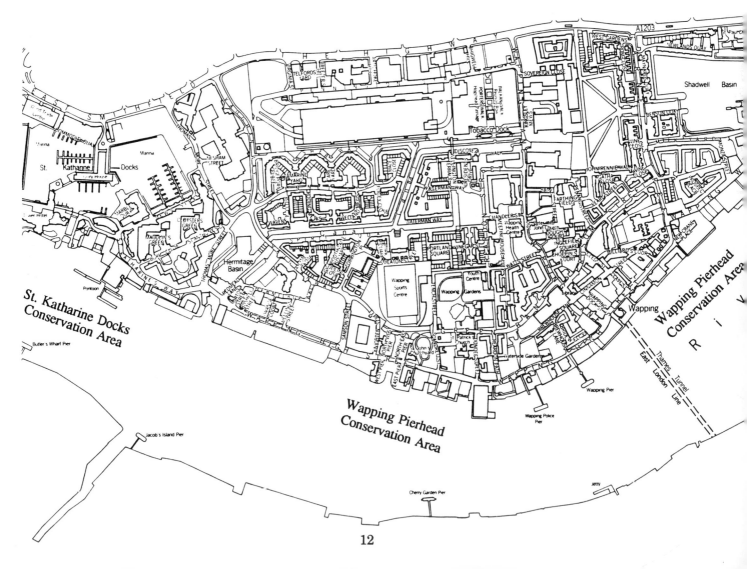

Riverside Walkways

Historically, public access to the River Thames in Wapping and most parts of Docklands was restricted by a continuous wall of wharves and warehouses, broken only by entrance locks and stairways to the river. In general most new developments and conversions in Wapping have provided public access to the riverside. These have been achieved through continuous jetties or arcaded walkways through the buildings. Continuous quayside access has been provided for the retained areas of Hermitage and Shadwell Basins, and the new canal which links through the filled basins of the Eastern and Western Docks. In Limehouse there is a riverside walkway along the length of the Free Trade Wharf and along Blyths' Wharf. Limehouse basin has been retained with moorings and recreational facilities.

St Katharine Docks

Perhaps St Katharine Docks, nestling in the shadow of Tower Bridge and the Tower of London, is the epitomy of success in London Docklands and an inspiration to others in the world. The yacht club, against the spectacle of Dickens Inn and Ivory House with its parade of fine shops, has become a shrine for Londoners and visitors from all over the globe.

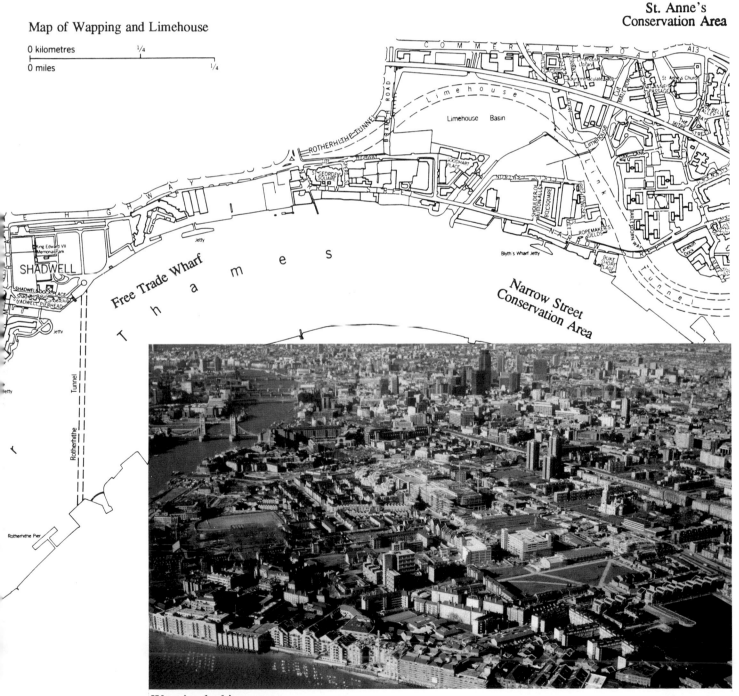

Map of Wapping and Limehouse

Wapping looking west

13

WAPPING AND LIMEHOUSE

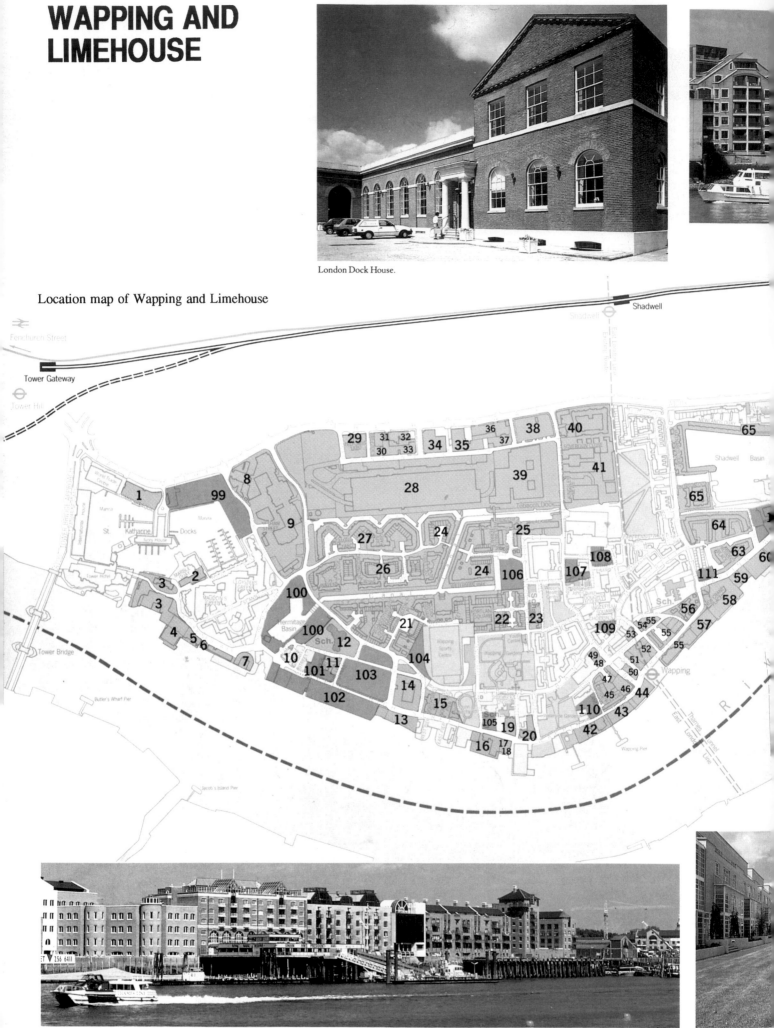

London Dock House.

Location map of Wapping and Limehouse

Wapping waterfront from Harrison & South Devon Wharfs to Tower Bridge Wharf.

Roy Square.

Middleton and St Brides Wharf.

Pelican Wharf.

River frontage including Metropolitan Wharf

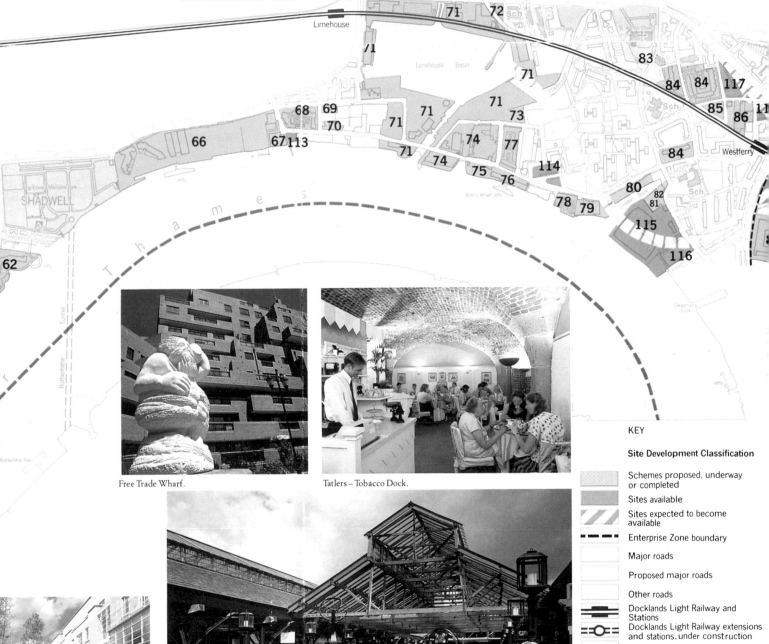

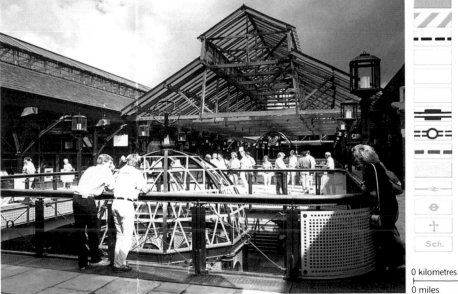

Free Trade Wharf.

Tatlers – Tobacco Dock.

Tobacco Dock.

KEY

Site Development Classification

Schemes proposed, underway or completed

Sites available

Sites expected to become available

Enterprise Zone boundary

Major roads

Proposed major roads

Other roads

Docklands Light Railway and Stations

Docklands Light Railway extensions and stations, under construction

River bus services

Parks, Public open space and recreational area

British Rail lines and stations

London Underground stations

Church

Sch.   School

0 kilometres   1/4

0 miles   1/4

LONDON DOCKLANDS
WAPPING AND LIMEHOUSE

LOCATION MAP FEATURE NUMBERS

The features described in this section of the book are numbered as listed below and the locations are shown by the corresponding numbers on the map on the preceeding page.

1.	Commodity Quay	51.	123 Wapping High Street	100.	Hermitage Basin
2.	Marble Quay	52.	125-131 Wapping High Street	101.	Orange Court
3.	Devon House	53.	R Warehouse, Cinnamon Street	102.	Hermitage Riverside
4.	Presidents Quay			103.	Hermitage Wall
5.	Millers Wharf	54.	S Warehouse, Cinnamon Street	104.	Knighten Street
6.	84 St Katharines Way			105.	Scandrett Street
7.	Tower Bridge Wharf	55.	Towerside and Prusom Island Warehouse	106.	East Quay 3
8.	London Dock House			107.	Raine Street
9.	Thomas More Street	56.	Garnet Street	108.	Farthing Fields
10.	Orton Street	57.	St. Hilda's Wharf	109.	Pruson Street/Choppins Court
11.	20-32 Hermitage Wall	58.	New Crane Wharf	110.	Brewhouse Lane
12.	New Primary School	59.	Jubilee and Luske Wharves	111.	Garnet Street/Wapping Wall
13.	Black Eagle Wharf	60.	Metropolitan Wharf	112.	London Hydraulic Power Station
14.	Hermitage Court	61.	Pelican Wharf		
15.	Wapping Pierhead	62.	Prospect Wharf	113.	14-16 Narrow Street
16.	Orient Wharf	63.	Prospect Place	114.	Brightlingsea Building Site
17.	78 Wapping High Street	64.	Riverside Mansions	115.	Dundee Wharf
18.	80 Wapping High Street	65.	Shadwell Basin	116.	Buchanans Wharf
19.	73 Wapping High Street	66.	Free Trade Wharf	117.	West India Dock Road Site
20.	75-79 Wapping High Street/1 Reardon Path	67.	Keepier Wharf	118.	West India Dock Road Site
		68.	St Georges Square	119.	Woolmore Street
21.	South Quay	69.	402-408 The Highway	120.	Garford Street Triangle
22.	East Quay 4	70.	Eagle Wharf	121.	Stoneyard Lane
23.	St. Peters School	71.	Limehouse Basin	122.	Poplar Fire Station
24.	East Quay 2	72.	618-620 Commercial Road		
25.	East Quay 1	73.	2-4 Northey Street		
26.	Western Dock Basin	74.	Houghs Papermill		
27.	Western Dock Basin	75.	Hough and Dover Wharves		
28.	News International	76.	Blyth's Wharf		
29.	Telfords Yard	77.	Roy Square		
30.	Breezers Hill	78.	98-100 Narrow Street		
31.	26-36 The Highway	79.	Duke Shore Wharf		
32.	Pennington Court	80.	Dunbar Wharf		
33.	Artichoke Hill	81.	Limekiln Wharf		
34.	100 The Highway	82.	90-96 Three Colt Street		
35.	110 Pennington Street	83.	Limehouse Church Institute		
36.	102-128 The Highway	84.	Roche Estate		
37.	122-132 Pennington Street	85.	Rich Street		
38.	130-162 The Highway	86.	Grenade Street		
39.	Tobacco Dock	87.	Cannon Workshops		
40.	172-176 The Highway	88.	Dockmasters House		
41.	Wapping Lane	89.	Hertsmere House		
42.	St. John's and King Henry's Wharves	90.	Port East		
43.	Gun House	91.	Shed 35		
44.	Gun Wharves	92.	Post 16 College		
45.	Bridewell Place	93.	Docklands Light Railway Depot		
46.	Gun Place	94.	New Cannon Workshops		
47.	Morgan House	95.	216-242 Poplar High Street		
48.	78-80 Wapping Lane	96.	260-268 Poplar High Street		
49.	70 Wapping Lane	97.	272-286 Poplar High Street		
50.	The Carronade	98.	Bazley Street/Cotton Street		
		99.	St Katharine Docks East Basin		

Note

Feature numbers 87 to 122 of the location map are situated within Poplar and West India Docks areas and are shown on pages 45 to 47.

Further Information

London Docklands
Development Corporation
Thames Quay
191 Marsh Wall
Isle of Dogs
London, E14 9TJ
Telephone: 071-512-3000

ST KATHARINE DOCKS CONSERVATION AREA

St Katharine By The Tower - The Jewel near the Crown

St Katharine by the Tower is a magnificent development at the western end of Docklands in the Tower Conservation Area. Tower Hill station of Docklands Light Railway is nearby. Being one of London's commercial and leisure complexes and rich in history and heritage, it encompasses some 12 hectares of land and water on the edge of the City and has beautiful views of the River and the adjacent historic Tower of London and Tower Bridge. There is a balanced thriving environment for tourists, business people and private residents. It was one of the first parts of Docklands to be re-developed in the early 1970s and is considered generally as one of the classical good examples of urban regeneration in the world.

The history of the site can be traced back to the 12th century when Queen Matilda built a Hospital and a Chapel of "St Katharine by the Tower" on this site to care for the sick and the poor. Over the years houses and narrow streets grew up around the church and by the early nineteenth century more than ten thousand people lived in the area. In 1827 the whole site was sold, and construction started on the Eastern and Western Docks.

The quayside warehouses were designed by the architect Philip Hardwick, and the docks were built by the engineer Thomas Telford. In the warehouses came a variety of imports including ivory, tea, spices, tobacco, sugar, indigo, marble and scent from all over the world, whilst in the vaults beneath the buildings were stored wines from Europe, Africa and Australia. The Ivory House was once the centre of the ivory trade in London and housed the raw material for thousands of piano keys and ornaments. St Katharine Docks traded for over 120 years but declined as ships increased in size, and no longer were able to pass through the lock into the basins. During the second world war bombs and fires destroyed large areas of the warehouses and quays, and in the 1960s there was a revolution in the shipping technology which eventually caused these and other London docks to be closed. Over the past two decades new construction and refurbishment have transformed the area into offices, luxury apartments and boating facilities.

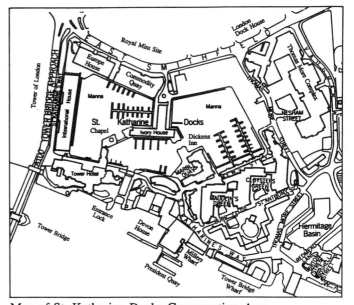

Map of St. Katharine Docks Conservation Area

St. Katharine Docks

Historic Tower of London

Adjacent to St Katharine Docks is the Tower of London which was built by William the Conqueror about 900 years ago as a royal palace and a fortress to defend London after the Battle of Hastings. Prior to 1675, it was used as an observatory by the genius astronomer Isaac Newton. As a prison it had famous inmates such as Sir Walter Raleigh and Sir Thomas More. The Tower was a famous execution site in medieval times. Nowadays it houses the Crown jewels and an armoury museum including those of King Henry VIII.

The World Trade Centre

The World Trade Centre is in St Katharine's Way, which runs parallel to the northern approach to Tower Bridge. The building, International House, is occupied by the World Trade Institute, World Trade Centre secretariat and services, and member companies of the London World Trade Centre Association. It is a replica of the old B warehouses, which previously stood on the site. They were stock brick with low hipped roofs, six storeys high, three blocks of six bays each, linked by four bay recessed sections with loopholes and jiggers over courtyards space.

The Tower Hotel

The riverside Tower Hotel, built in 1973, is situated next to the International World Trade Centre and has superb views of the Thames. The hotel was built on the site of St. Katharine tea Warehouse and Irongate Wharf next to Tower Bridge. The wharf was used by the General Steam Navigation Company which operated regular services to European Ports. It had bonded floors for spirits and wine. The company also operated pleasure trips from Tower Pier on the west side of the bridge. The Tower Hotel is an international tourist centre with its own restaurant overlooking the Docks and their colourful yachts.

St Katharine's Yacht Haven

Opened in 1973, St Katharine is the only yacht haven in the heart of London, with moorings for yachts and motor boats. One of the historic crafts in the haven, is the Massey Shaw, a London fire float which fought dock and warehouse fires during the blitz in the second world war. Another craft is the S.S. Yarmouth which ferried passengers between Yarmouth and Gorleston before the first world war. The Lady Daphne is a Thames spritsail barge built at Rochester in 1923 and has been restored for charter work.

Europe House

On the north side of the West Basin there is a business community centred in offices at Europe House which was built by the Port of London Authority in the 1960s. Previously it was used by The PLA for dock accounts and finance as well as housing the Chief Police Department.

The World Trade Centre

The Tower of London

Tower Hotel, Ivory House and Dockmaster's House

Commodity Quay

Commodity Quay is a modern office block adjacent to Europe House on the north quayside housing the London Commodity Exchange. It was built in 1987 on the site of old "C" warehouses. [1]

Thames Sailing Barge Races

The Thames Sailing Barges have held annual races for well over one hundred years. During the years that the barges were used in the London docks and wharves there was immense competition between owners and crews to win for the sake of their company's name. As the docks started to close in the late 1960s the demand for cargo carrying vessels fell and so did the glorious sight of racing barges. Today, enthusiasts still organize barge matches for fun. The matches take place along the Thames and the south east coast line.

Ivory House

The listed Ivory House, the centrepiece of the conservation area, was built in 1854. The original cast iron columns, brick facade and vaulted ceilings, have been retained in the restoration. The Italianate style building, designed by Aitcheson, was once the centre of London's ivory trade. Exclusive apartments have been created, overlooking the Yacht Haven, which with the rest of the development is floodlit at night. The Ivory House also includes offices, shops and the Beefeater Restaurants, which stages medieval entertainment and feasts in the vaults. The warehouse building is T shaped on plan, four storeys high with stock brick, and arched windows. There is a bell turret and a semi-circular arched arcade which leads to the ground floor and the vaulted basement.

Telford Bridge

The iron footbridge between Marble Quay and Ivory House was designed and built by Telford in 1829. Manually operated, the leaves withdraw under the quay so that boats can pass between the central basin and the east dock. The structure is the oldest moveable bridge in Docklands and one of the oldest surviving wrought iron bridges in England. A new bridge is set to replace it but will incorporate many of the original features of the existing structure.

Marble Quay

This is an extension of Dickens Inn development providing residential and commercial accommodation on the former quay of the Eastern Basin where ships used to unload marble from Italy. [2]

Ivory House shops with iron pillars

The old sailing barges race

Ivory House and the Thames barge "Lady Daphne"

The Dickens Inn

This public house is part of the old G Warehouse which was situated on the south side of St. Katharine Docks. A 200-year old timber building was found encased in the bricks of the warehouse which had to be demolished. The original building was built 1793-99 and later remodelled and altered during 1828-38 by Hardwick. Part of the frame was moved bodily in 1974 to the present site to form The Dickens Inn. The interior is old but the external casing of the building is wholly modern.

The Chapel

The circle of seven cast-iron doric columns from one of the former warehouses encloses an altar surmounted by a large slab of Perspex. This represents the Imperial Crown against the rays of the sun. The small chapel stands virtually on the same site as did the Church of St Katharine, which was demolished to make way for the dock.

Dockmaster's House and Swing Bridge

The 19th century swing bridge across the lock entrance to St Katharine's has been replaced by a new steel lifting bridge at one end and a Dutch timber lifting bridge near the river. The former Dockmaster's House, built 1830 to the east of the entrance, is fully restored and in residential use.

South Quay Housing

The development on the south quay of the Eastern Basin includes 300 homes built for the former Greater London Council. A pedestrian walkway links the whole of the scheme at the second floor and each of the blocks has its own roofed street at a higher level.

The Dickens Inn

The Chapel, Commodity Quay and Ivory House

DEVON HOUSE AND PRESIDENT QUAY

The Tower Conservation Area

The part of the Tower Conservation Area which lies within London Docklands north of the Thames stretches from Tower Bridge to Thomas More Street and includes the whole of the St. Katharine Docks, St. Katharine's Way and the old entrance to Hermitage Basin. Rebuilding along the riverfront has been completed and consists of Devon House, President Quay, Millers Wharf, 84 St. Katharine Way and Tower Bridge Wharf.

Devon House

St. Katharine's Way leads from St. Katharine Docks on to Wapping High Street. Devon House, originally earmarked as the UK location of the European Trade Mark Office, is the first riverside development in St Katharine's Way, east of the lock entrance with views of Tower Bridge and complete with a water garden plaza. The building, adjoining the old Dockmaster's House, is on the site of the old South Devon Wharf which had a range of two storey warehouses of early 19th century construction for discharge of tea and wool from lighters. [3]

President Quay

The President Quay, adjacent to Devon House on St Katharine Way, comprises riverside apartments and four penthouses, built around a landscaped atrium on four levels above the headquarters of the Royal Naval Reserve, HMS President. The impressive atrium is beautifully landscaped with trees, shrubs and cascading water. These riverside apartments set the scene for the nautical theme. The building derives its name from HMS President, once a ship of the line, now the title of the Royal Naval Reserve's London Division, which occupies the lower three floors. The original warehouse and jetty were the terminal of the P&O Jetfoil Service. Appropriately the rebuilt complex is by Bovis Homes, part of the P&O Group since 1974. There are porthole and warehouse type of windows, ship-style railings in the passages and balconies. There is a compass motif on the entrance hall carpet. [4]

Millers Wharf

This is a beautiful conversion of a Grade 2 listed riverside warehouse adjacent to President Quay. In the old days all types of non-bonded cargo were handled and stored as required from barges at the wharf. [5]

Devon House, President Quay and Millers Wharf

TOWER BRIDGE WHARF AND HERMITAGE BASIN

84 St. Katharine's Way

This is an architecturally modern riverside office building adjacent to Millers Wharf. The external treatment of the building, which is a mix of aluminium cladding coated with white stoved polyester powder and dark-tinted heat-absorbent glass, makes it a contrast with the traditional warehouse buildings of the area.   [6]

Tower Bridge Wharf

Tower Bridge Wharf is an apartment complex to the east of 84 St Katharine Way, which looks out over the Thames to the historic Butlers Wharf. Its nautical location is reflected in glossy red metalwork against the ochre brickwork, blue-grey slate roofing and lighter grey stone elevations. The chimney cappings are stone-clad and the balconies have poppy red balustrades. The development fronts a walkway and jetty on St. Katharine Way and is on the site of Carrvon and Continental Steam Wharves. The old wharves had a massive six storey warehouse for handling cargoes including tea and wines. Fruit and vegetables were also discharged for Covent Garden. The Carrvon Company owned the wharves and operated a regular service between London and Glasgow.
[7]

Hermitage Basin

The basin was built in 1805 as part of the old London Docks complex and as part of redevelopment it has been partly filled to reduce its depth from 10m to 1.5m. A new waterside square has been created with a public walkway along the quayside. The former impounding pump house has been converted into a sculptor's studio.

Hermitage Entrance

The London dock system was originally the Western Dock with two connecting basins - Wapping and Hermitage - each connecting the dock with an entrance to the Thames. The Hermitage Entrance was used by barges, lighters and small ships. The Port of London Authority closed the entrance in 1909.

Hermitage Court

Across the old entrance to the London Docks and along Wapping High Street is Hermitage Court. The development combines refurbishment of an old Victorian spice house and a former printing works, with newly built wings which link them to provide apartments, shops and offices.   [14]

Tower Bridge Wharf looking west

LONDON DOCK HOUSE AND THOMAS MORE STREET

Old Dock Walls

At the eastern boundary of the Tower Conservation Area lies Thomas More Street, with the historic London Dock House and some remaining sections of the original 19th century London Docks security boundary walls. They are about 5m high and are stock brick loping and some with vermiculated stone bonding.

London Dock House

London Dock House is the oldest dock offices in the world. The two buildings, designed in 1805 by Daniel Alexander, the Surveyor to the London Docks Company housed the Custom & Excise Offices and were used by the Port of London Authority until 1985, when it was sold for redevelopment. The entrance and gates on the corner of East Smithfield and Thomas More Street were the main entrance to the London Docks. The forecourt of the north building has been repaved with granite sets. The Portland stone portico is entirely new and incorporates an original pattern Georgian fanlight. The windows were replaced with double hung sashes to match the originals. [8]

Thomas More Street

This complex, past the London Dock House, includes six office blocks, the highest being 13 storeys, residential apartments, shops and a sports centre. The white marble buildings are mostly four and five storeys with the 13 storey block acting as the central point of the project. Access to the office complex is from a main piazza which features entrances into each individual building with atria in the principal blocks.

The new buildings have been erected on the site of the demolished warehouses of the old London Docks. The main entrance to the Docks led to a broad road running between the tall warehouses where wine casks used to lay and be attended to by Custom Officers, gaugers and samplers. Past the Dock House buildings was the famous No.6 Warehouse which stored wool, eastern spices and ivory tusks from Africa and Asia. In the basements were the wine vaults. [9]

Thomas More Court

This is a development of two to four bedroom homes set along the banks of a tree lined canal close to St. Katharine Docks.

London Dock House

Thomas More Street office complex

WESTERN BASIN AND NEWS INTERNATIONAL

Old London Docks

When the London Docks in Wapping were built at the beginning of the 19th century, many buildings and homes were demolished to make way for the basins and the quayside warehouses. In the early 1980s history was reversed; for the dock basins were filled and the warehouses were demolished for complete redevelopment of the area into over 1000 new homes and the large printing works of News International. The reclaimed Western Dock subdivides into three main housing developments - the Western Basin, East Quay and South Quay. The central feature of the development is the new Canal which is a surface water reservoir as well as being an attractive amenity.

The London Dock Company was established in 1800 and had a 21-year monopoly on all ships carrying tobacco, rice, brandy and wine into the Port of London. The Western Dock was completed in 1806, followed by the Tobacco Dock in 1814. The Eastern Dock was opened later in 1828. The warehouses stored numerous commodities including spices, ivory, silk, cotton, coffee, dried fruits and nuts. In the extensive vaults below the warehouses wine and brandy were kept. The docks were closed in 1968 following the moving of the Port of London to deep coastal water at Tilbury.

Western Basin

The history of the Western Basin is recalled in the names of the various parts of this new development of over 300 homes. There is Trade Winds Court, Tamarind Yard, Spice Court, etc. The buildings look on to landscaped gardens within four crescent-shaped courtyards. [27]

Waterman Quay

This canalside development has a variety of flats and houses in South Quay. The development has views of the St George in the East church and the River Thames. [21]

East Quay

East Quay is set alongside the historic Tobacco Dock, and contains homes which lie behind the original brick walls of the Victorian warehouse. Trees have been planted to line the Quay walkway. [24]

Western Basin housing

Wapping showing Western Basin, News International, Tobacco Dock and Shadwell Basin

News International Print Works

The new printing complex was built in Pennington Street, the site of the old warehouses along the north quay of the Western Dock. The five warehouses, called stacks, were designed by Daniel Alexander c1804 and were demolished in the late 1970s to make way for the printing works. The press hall, currently printing over four million newspaper copies every night, forms the largest operation in the world. The four titles are The Times, Sunday Times, News of the World and The Sun. [28]

Pennington Court

A new residential development located in Pennington Street. The upper floor apartments are known as "Sun Galleries" with their south-facing floor-to-ceiling windows. [33]

Telfords Yard

A Victorian warehouse conversion that is north of News International and close to the Highway. The apartments have original brickwork and high ceilings built in 1882. Telfords Yard was one of the first warehouses to be converted in Docklands. [29]

Church of St. George in the East

The Church of St. George in the East, in a conservation area on the north side of The Highway at Wapping, is an English Baroque architectural masterpiece dating from the early 18th century. It was renovated and cleaned in 1983. It is located opposite Tobacco Dock Shopping Precinct and is only a few minutes walk from Shadwell Station of Docklands Light Railway.

Telfords Yard

The Church of St. George in the East

TOBACCO DOCK CONSERVATION AREA

Tobacco Dock Shopping Precinct

Near to the Tower of London stands one of the most exciting business developments in the world, the Tobacco Dock Shopping Precinct. It is located close to the Shadwell Station of Docklands Light Railway. It is also within walking distance of Wapping Tube Station. Built in 1814 with massive vaults to store hogshead of tobacco, brandy, rum and sherry, the historic Tobacco Dock, a Grade 1 listed building, is a unique and the best preserved example of the 19th century engineering and architecture. It is well known for its structural innovation and is one of the earliest uses of cast iron in the world. The fine bays of the original warehouse form a massive family leisure and shopping complex over an area of five acres with no supporting walls between the bays. Huge timber roof trusses span nearly 18 metres (54ft) between cast iron stanchions. Below ground floor level are three acres of vaults with granite pillars. Today, the shopping precinct, twice the size of Covent Garden, is below areas of open glass roof leading to the creation of basement courts and first floor galleries with large stores, bar and restaurants. The cellar level has been turned into a network of small shops and malls. The shops occupy the vaults between adjacent columns and they have cast iron window frames and doors with ornamental brackets and signs in front of each shop re-creating a Dickensian atmosphere of London. Extensive use of cast ironwork has been made throughout the development to complement the cast iron stanchions and other original features of the building.   [39]

Treasure Island Pirate Ships

Two replica sailing ships are housed along the quayside of the shopping complex to re-create the old docklands environment and to act as a major tourist attraction. They are replicas of the original vessels the "Three Sisters" and "The Sea Lark" which were built in the 18th century. The two ships are typical examples of the ships which traded in the London Docks early 1800. The "Three Sisters" traded in tobacco regularly between Tobacco Dock, the West Indies and other parts of the world. A merchantship of 330 tons, she was built at Blackwall Yard of docklands in 1788. The "Sea Lark", was originally an American built schooner which was later acquired by the Admiralty.

Sovereign Court

Sovereign Court is a Georgian Style development of six self-contained two and three storey workshop buildings in a mews setting. It is located opposite Tobacco Dock on the site of the Eastern Basin of the old London Docks in Wapping.   [41]

Tobacco Dock shopping precinct and replica ships

Tobacco Dock Dickensian Vaults

WAPPING PIERHEAD CONSERVATION AREA

Wapping Pierhead Area

This conservation area, an attractive part of Docklands, covers both sides of Wapping High Street from Wapping Pierhead to Wapping Station. Most of the former warehouses and buildings along the river frontage are Grade 2 listed and have been beautifully renovated as luxury apartments. These include the Georgian Houses on either side of the filled-in lock, and listed warehouses such as Olivers Wharf, St. John's Wharf and Gun Wharves next to Wapping Station.

St. John's Church

Off Wapping High Street and along Scandrett Street is the Tower of St. Johns. The church was designed by Johnson in 1756, but was severely damaged by bombing during the war in 1940 and now only its tower, topped by a cupola, remains.

St. Patrick's Church

The Roman Catholic Church was designed by Tasker and built in 1879. It lies to the east of St. John's Church and has a beautiful Victorian marble altar.

Black Eagle Wharf

This is a residential development located west of Wapping Pierhead, all overlooking the river and Tower Bridge. The old wharf on the same site was mainly used for handling casks of Truman's beer with their sign of the black eagle.   [13]

Wapping Pierhead Houses

These attractive Georgian houses, three storeys high, were built between 1811-1813 for dock officials and were designed by Daniel Alexander, the Surveyor to the London Docks Company. The terraces were on each side of Wapping entrance which has been filled in. These houses and the adjoining Victorian Olivers Wharf were the first buildings converted into luxury homes in Docklands early in the 1970s.

To the east of these houses lie Wapping Old Stairs which is approached by a narrow passage from Wapping High Street. Access to the river by watermen and their passengers was by means of such stairs which led down to stone hards built out to the low watermark.

Black Eagle Wharf, Wapping Pierhead and Olivers Wharf

Georgian Houses of Wapping Pierhead

Town of Ramsgate Public House

This riverside Public House, in a corner of Oliver's Wharf, claims to have been the last stop for "Hanging Judge Jeffries" before the Tower of London! Legends say that he was caught in this alehouse in 1688 by an infuriated mob whilst trying to escape to France. The pub was named after the boats from Ramsgate which brought fish to London and moored nearby. Ramsgate Harbour of 1850 is featured on the pub sign.

Oliver's Wharf

Oliver's Wharf was the first warehouse conversion into flats in Docklands. The beautiful red brick Victorian riverside building was built in 1870 in Gothic style for a merchant George Oliver. For a hundred years it handled general cargo and tea.

Orient Wharf

Further along Wapping High Street is a residential development on the site of the old tea warehouses of Orient Wharf. The clock tower and steeple of St. Johns Church are in the background. [16]

78/80 Wapping High Street

These are typical red brick Victorian riverside Wharves originally built in 1830. In 1934 they were occupied by R G Hall & Co and were used for the storage of general dry goods such as coffee, cocoa, sugar, dried and canned fruit, gums and cheese. Oddbins moved into the wharves in 1976 for their offices with the warehouse on the other side of Wapping Lane being used as their wine warehouse. Human bones were discovered during refurbishment in the 1980s which were believed to be the remains of a murder victim. The riverside building is used as offices. [17]

The Town of Ramsgate Public House in Wapping High Street

Church of St. John

Oliver's Wharf, Orient Wharf with St. John's Church spire in the background, and 78/80 Wapping High Street

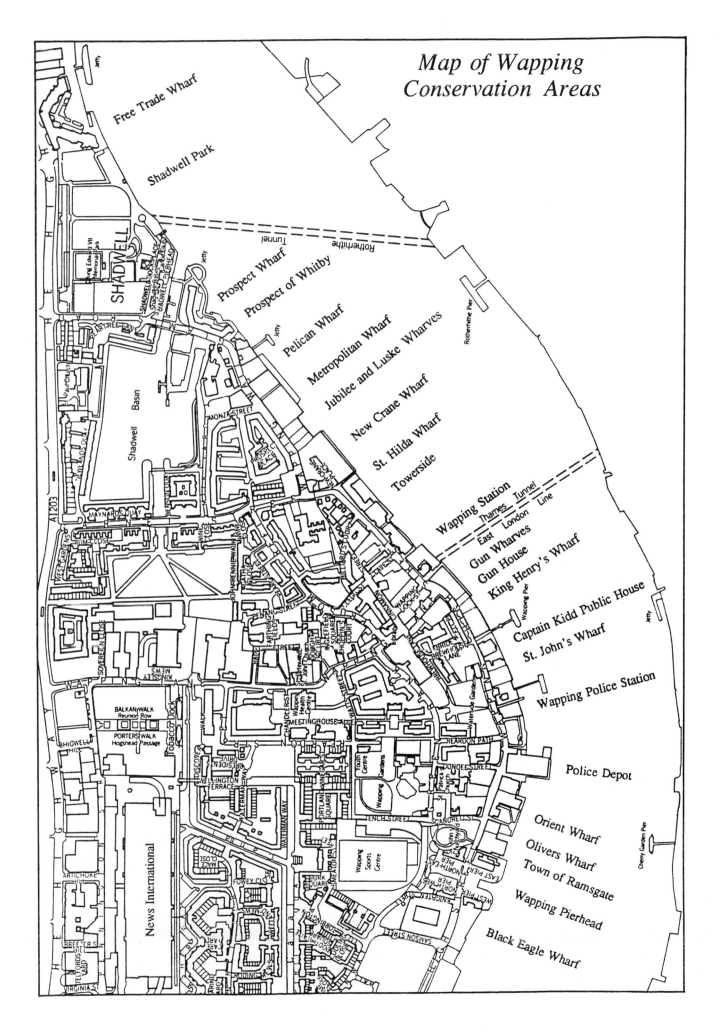

Map of Wapping
Conservation Areas

29

ST JOHN'S WHARF AND KING HENRY'S WHARF

Wapping Police Station and Museum

The modern riverside headquarters of the Thames Division of the Metropolitan Police, stands on the site of the old station, built in 1797 to house the first River Police force in the world. Early this century the site was also occupied by Morocco Wharf. Inside the Police Station there is a small museum which contains old documents, equipment and uniforms of the River Police. It is open to visitors by appointment; lectures and guided tours can be arranged.

To the west of the station past the small park is a single storey depot and workshop opened in 1973 for the maintenance of police launches. Clad in moulded glass reinforced plastic white panels, the building is quite prominent from the river. A special lift raises the boats into the workshop at all water levels.

St. John's Wharf

St. John's Wharf, adjacent to Wapping Police Station, is a beautiful warehouse conversion. The red brick Victorian wharf, was formerly used for storage of coffee, dried fruit and gum. For a period the Wharf was used for Australian wool sales. This stretch of river frontage was occupied by the Alexander Tug Company and was used for the storage of their supplies and maintenance of their Sun tug fleet. It was known as the "Sun Hole"! **[42]**

Captain Kidd Public House

The ground and first floors of the warehouse adjoining the new St. John's Wharf are occupied by a riverside public house "Captain Kidd" with exposed restored timber and warehouse relics. It is close to the old Execution Dock where Captain Kidd and other pirates of the 17th century came to a dead end!

King Henry's Wharf

This group of beautiful warehouses was owned by the Alexander Tug Company but operated by Hall Wharfingers who also were based at St. John's Wharf. The wharf was used primarily for handling and storage of sugar and coffee. Bonded facilities under the direction of the Custom Officers were available. The Grade 2 listed buildings, on each side of Wapping Pier, are awaiting redevelopment. **[42]**

Wapping Police Station, St. John's Wharf and Captain Kidd Public House

GUN WHARVES CONSERVATION AREA

Gun Wharves and Place

This superb residential conversion of Grade 2 listed Victorian buildings adjacent to Wapping Tube Station in a conservation area has magnificent apartments, providing unrivalled views of the River Thames. Some have private roof terraces and gardens. Built during the second half of the 19th century, the wharves were used for handling of tea, canned goods, hides and skins, caskwork and general cargo. Gun House is a new small development adjacent to Gun Wharves, which consists of nine luxury apartments. Gun Place, the Grade 2 listed former tea and spice warehouse opposite Gun Wharves, was also converted into luxury flats and penthouses. [44]

The Carronade

The Carronade is a small residential building which is situated opposite Wapping Underground Station, at the corner of Wapping High Street and Wapping Lane. The apartments are approached via an atrium entrance hall with an open curved staircase. There is a full size replica of a Carronade Naval Gun (circa 1805) as a fascinating centre piece and may prove to be a deterrent to unwelcome visitors! [50]

Wapping Tube Station

The tunnel which carries the East London Line under the Thames was the first tunnel for public transport to be driven beneath a river. It was designed by Sir Marc Isambard Brunel and constructed during the period 1825 to 1843. His son Isambard Kingdom Brunel was the engineer in charge from 1825 to 1828. Wapping Station was built at the site of the original shaft and the lifts were constructed within the iron framework of the shaft. The tube line runs from Shoreditch to New Cross with stations at Whitechapel, Shadwell, Wapping, Rotherhithe and Surrey Docks. (See page 102 for Brunel Pumphouse Museum).

Bridewell Place

Bridewell Place was an old soap factory adjoining Gun Place, which has been converted into apartments including galleried duplex flats and maisonettes. The Georgian style mews has its own courtyard and is close to Wapping Tube Station. [46]

Wapping Station, Towerside and St. Hilda's Wharf

Gun Place and Gun Wharves

NEW CRANE WHARF AND METROPOLITAN WHARF

Wapping Wall Conservation Area

This conservation area covers the eastern part of Wapping Wall and the entrance to Shadwell Basin. The two major historic warehouses which have been renovated and converted into residential and commercial units are the New Crane Wharf and the Metropolitan Wharf. Within this area are also the listed London Hydraulic Pumping Station with the adjoining Engineer's House. The new residential blocks along the river front are Towerside, Prospect Wharf and Pelican Wharf. Wapping and Shadwell Stations are close.

Towerside

Towerside is a riverside development in Wapping High Street to the east of Wapping Station. They are on the site of Middleton and St Brides Wharf. The apartments have beautiful views of the Thames to Surrey Docks. The exterior of the complex is designed in five towers of differing heights and varied brick finishes. **[55]**

St. Hilda's Wharf

St. Hilda's Wharf is a new residential development of 39 apartments adjacent to Towerside with similar architectural features. **[57]**

New Crane Wharf

This scheme is a beautiful conversion of three listed Victorian warehouses surrounding a cobbled courtyard to provide a mix of commercial and residential units between Wapping Wall and the River Thames. The units range from studios to three bedroom penthouses as well as shops, a health club and restaurant. **[58]**

Metropolitan Wharf

Metropolitan Wharf on Wapping's riverside was the first building to be listed by the London Docklands Development Corporation. The beautiful Victorian tea warehouse has been converted and is home to about 150 small firms. **[60]**

New Crane Wharf along Wapping Wall

Metropolitan Wharf

PELICAN WHARF AND PROSPECT WHARF

Pelican Wharf

At the eastern end of Wapping Wall Conservation Area, Pelican Wharf is a development of apartments with river frontage and with their own private floating river terrace and deep water moorings. Located nearby is the famous landmark of the London Hydraulic Pumping Station and Shadwell Basin, which is an area rich in history and tradition. During the 19th century, Pelican Wharf was the site of a barge building industry and later became a barge yard for storage of sand and ballast. [61]

The Prospect of Whitby Public House

Adjoining Pelican Wharf is the 16th century hostel and famous public house, said to be the oldest in London, boasting Judge Jeffries, Charles Dickens and Samuel Pepys among its patrons. The terrace has beautiful views of the River and the south bank. It is named after a collier called the Prospect which originally carried coal from Whitby in Yorkshire to the Wapping Hydraulic Power Station just to the north of the pub.

Prospect Wharf

Prospect Wharf is a complex of riverside apartments on a site which was once used for storage and treatment of timber to service the wharves on Millwall Outer Dock. This residential development fronts Shadwell outer lock and is adjacent to the Prospect of Whitby. The elevations are in light coloured London stock brick with contrasting darker brickwood at high and low levels. The pitched roof is designed along traditional warehouse lines. A brick wall separates the buildings grounds from the riverside walk. The Dockmasters residence and office were formerly along this river frontage.

The "noon-dial" anchor, positioned to identify mid-day in both Greenwich Mean Time and British Summer Time, is a striking feature in the development courtyard. The 2.1 tonnes iron "Admiralty Anchor" designed in 1841 by Sir John Parker was discovered in a marine scrapyard in Portsmouth. [62]

Pelican Wharf, Prospect of Whitby Public House and Prospect Wharf

Prospect of Whitby Public House

SHADWELL BASIN AND LONDON HYDRAULIC POWER STATION

Shadwell Basin

In 1853 an Act of Parliament was passed for the construction of a new Shadwell entrance and basin of much greater dimensions than the old one c 1831. The works were completed in 1858 and allowed bigger ships to enter the London Docks. This basin is today the only surviving dock of the London Docks. Waterside housing has been built around the basin, which is used as a water sports training centre for young people under the direction of the East London Marine Venture. The red painted old steel bascule bridges at Glamis Road and Garnet Street were constructed in the early 1930s and have been preserved across the basin. DLR Shadwell Station and Wapping Underground Station are nearby.

London Hydraulic Power Station

The London Hydraulic Power Company built their world wide famous pumping station in 1892 on the westside of Shadwell Basin. The red brick Grade 2 listed building with a fine accummulator tower has been a local landmark for a century. Coal was delivered to the adjacent Shadwell Basin and water was obtained from the same dock. Steam pumps were used to pump the water under pressure into the two accumulators. The steam plant was replaced by electric pumps in the 1950s due to the introduction of a smokeless zone in London and the station was put on the public water mains. It was closed in

1977 and since then several proposals have been suggested for its conversion into a studio and a home for the St Martin Orchestra. To the east of the building is the former residence of the Engineer for the power station.   [112]

The London Hydraulic Pumping Station overlooking Shadwell Basin

Shadwell Basin showing the new housing, St. Paul's Church and other landmarks

Shadwell Basin Housing

Shadwell Basin is a new residential development including flats and maisonettes and a range of houses from two to five bedrooms in a variety of architectural styles. Arranged around three sides of the historic dock, the majority of the properties have delightful water views and water sports facilities. Approached either from Glamis Road or Garnet Street off the Highway, Shadwell Basin is entered through an impressive archway. The visual impact is heightened by the vast expanse of enclosed water in the dock. The style of the architecture is given continuity in a series of arched colonnades and juxtaposed pitched roofs. Areas of brightly coloured curtain walling between traditional brick facing are highlighted by contrasting colours on the window frames and balconies. A stretch of old dock wall shelters the development from the Highway. The local historic church of St. Paul's is adjacent to the development. [65]

Shadwell Basin Sport Centre for sailing and canoeing

St. Paul's Church Conservation Area

This small conservation area is centred around St. Paul's Church circa 1821 and includes a row of early 19th century cottages facing the churchyard which have been restored as private residences. A flight of steps leads from the churchyard to the quayside of Shadwell Basin. The church has a railed wall, railings and massive iron gates with square piers and lamp brackets above each one.

Shadwell Park

This park, also known as King Edward VII Memorial Park, is a pleasant riverside garden opened in 1922 as a recreation area among the busy wharves of the then Port of London Authority. It has fine views of Rotherhithe and the Isle of Dogs. Notice the ventilation and access shaft of the Rotherhithe Tunnel. It is Grade 2 listed and has spiral stairs down to the tunnel which terminates at Rotherhithe on the south bank of the river.

Glamis Road lifting bridge across Shadwell Basin entrance lock

FREE TRADE WHARF CONSERVATION AREA

Free Trade Wharf and Mall

Free Trade Wharf is an attractive conservation area with riverside residential development adjacent to Shadwell Park. It was built in 1793 for the East India Company and it was originally designed for storing saltpetre. This is one of the main constituents of gunpowder. One of the two remaining 45ft Thames sailing barges which were used for transporting gunpowder has been installed on the site in an old barge dock where it has become an attraction of the riverside walkway. The original buildings on the wharf consisted of two parallel ranges of beautiful listed Georgian warehouses. As part of the development, these were refurbished and converted into six flats, seven shops, a wine bar, a restaurant, seven office suites and a leisure suite including a swimming pool. The Mall has a wide paved precinct which runs from the gated archway entrance through to the river walkway.   [66]

Free Trade Wharf West

From The Mall, the landscaped riverside walk leads to the new Free Trade Wharf West. Here ziggurat terraces build up from ground floor apartments with garden terraces to tenth storey penthouses, some topped with conservatories. Every flat has a balcony with southerly aspects and river views. There are sculptures along the river, the most dominant being Polly Ionides' Father Thames.

The House They Left Behind Public House

The Public House was built in 1857 and affectionately restored in 1985. It is literally left behind as it was part of a Victorian terrace which has been demolished. It has been re-named The Black Horse.

Keepier Wharf

This is a residential warehouse conversion at the junction of The Highway and Narrow Street in Limehouse with south facing views across the River Thames.   [67]

The Mall at Free Trade Wharf looking north.

Free Trade Wharf

LIMEHOUSE BASIN CONSERVATION AREAS

Limehouse Conservation Areas

Limehouse is centred upon Limehouse Basin and includes the Narrow Street and St Anne's Limehouse Conservation Areas. This is one of the older parts of East London. The Limehouse Basin was constructed in 1812 to serve barges at the end of Regents Canal. It was enlarged in 1820 to take sea vessels which carried coal to London. The Limehouse Basin connects the Regents Canal and the Limehouse Cut, part of the Grand Union Canal, with the River Thames. It reaches the river through a lock which was refurbished in the mid 1980s. The Blackwall Railway was built in 1838-40 and its brick viaduct on the north side of Limehouse Basin remains and is used by Docklands Light Railway. Decorative cast iron parapeting and heavy keystones enrich the Grade 2 listed viaduct. The architecture of the whole area is partly eighteenth century but mostly industrial nineteenth century. The nineteenth century warehouses around Limekiln Dock are well preserved.

Limehouse Basin

This is a redevelopment of the redundant dockland around the basin with housing and public amenities including water sports. The houses have been built in coloured bricks with tiled roofs and timber verandas overlooking the water and the entrance lock. [71]

Limehouse Link Road

Since 1989, considerable progress has been made in the construction of the new 1.8 km Limehouse Link road. The four-lane route is contained entirely in tunnel with an underground junction part-way along its length. It runs beneath the north side of Limehouse Basin before swinging south towards the Isle of Dogs. When complete in 1993, the road will link The Highway, at the junction of Butcher Row and Narrow Street, to Westferry Road. (see page 131)

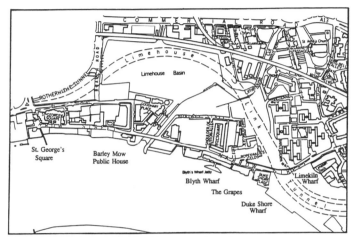

Map of Limehouse Basin Conservation Areas

Limehouse Basin

37

The Barley Mow Public House

The London brewer Taylor Walker first started brewing near this site c.1730 at its Barley Mow brewery. This pub, opened in 1989, is the conversion of the original 19th century Dockmaster's house at the entrance to Limehouse Basin. The pub has a huge open space on the bank of the Thames, providing views of development along the river.

The Limehouse Cut Canal

The Regent's Canal, which opened in 1820, linked the Port of London with England's inland waterways via Limehouse Basin. Earlier in 1770 the Limehouse Cut to the east of Limehouse Basin, had been built to link the River Lea with the Thames.

Limehouse Cut Wharf

The Limehouse Cut Wharf, one-time Spratt's dog-biscuits and Coleman's Mustard warehouses, was converted in 1989 into live-and-work units for artists and studios. There are studios for pottery, textile and advertising. The conversion of warehouses dating back to 1895 stands as a landmark in the East End overlooking the old Limehouse Cut Canal.

St. Anne's Church Conservation Area

St. Anne's Church, easily approached from Commercial Road, was built in 1712-14 and a small number of houses in the area survive from the same period. The architecture is the same as that for St. George in the East church. Its clock face was made in the same workshop which provided Big Ben's face. The church's prized Victorian organ was the winner of the Great Exhibition of 1851. Westferry and Limehouse Stations of DLR are nearby.

St. Anne's Church

Limehouse Cut Wharf

The Barley Mow Public House

BLYTH WHARF AND DUKE SHORE WHARF

Narrow Street Conservation Area

Narrow Street is situated in Limehouse, known in the eighteenth century as the Hamlet of Ratcliff, and has always been associated with shipping and trade. Dickens, whose father worked in the area, was a regular visitor and the atmosphere and characters provided the inspiration for a number of his books, including Dombey and Son, while living in Narrow Street. The street has a group of former Captains' and merchants' houses by the Grapes public house which have been restored and are rather unique in London. The predominant facing material is brick with some render on the merchants' houses. Limehouse Station is within few minutes walk.

Blyth's Wharf

Blyth's Wharf, at the western end of Narrow Street, is a new riverside residential development of three and four storey houses on the site of old coal wharves for Stepney Power Station. The development archway leads on to the jetty with its public open space. Designed to match the adjacent 18th century ship Captains' houses, Blyth's Wharf was once bustling with schooners from the North of England, including the port of Blyth, unloading cargoes of coal. The residents of Limehouse were used to the sights and sounds of every kind of boat along the Thames, including the London sailing barges with their large sails, crewed just by two men. Blyth's Wharf houses have been finished in London yellow bricks.   [76]

Roy Square

Facing Blyth's Wharf, Roy Square is a large residential development around a courtyard with waterscape features.

[77]

The Grapes Public House and former Captain Houses in Narrow Street

Narrow Street showing Blyth Wharf, Roy Square, The Grapes and Duke Short Wharf

The Grapes Public House

This listed old pub is adjacent to Blyth's Wharf and enjoys beautiful views of the river and Limehouse conservation area. Here Dickens used to sit and get his inspiration for writing the novel "Our Mutual Friend". The fish restaurant, situated upstairs, has its specialties straight from the nearby Billingsgate Market. There is a Victorian style bar downstairs.

Duke Shore Wharf

This is a riverside residential development at the eastern side of Narrow Street. There is an adjacent stair and a small dock which was used for barge repairs. **[79]**

Limekiln Wharf

At the eastern end of Narrow Street is the listed Limekiln Dock, which was an old pottery site dating back to the 17th century. Limekiln Wharf is a conversion of a group of listed warehouses which overlook the old dock. It consists of two adjoining sites, at the junction of Narrow Street and Colts Street, on one of which 6 flats and a shop were built, and 23 flats and one commercial unit were built on the other site. The warehouses along Narrow Street, form part of Dunbar Wharf named after the 19th century ship owner, Duncan Dunbar. **[81]**

The Grapes Public House

Limekiln Wharf

Narrow Street looking east

ISLE OF DOGS

The New City

By the year 2000 the new city on the Isle of Dogs will be very different from the old City of London. The three towers of Canary Wharf standing as the tallest group of buildings in Europe will dominate London's skyline. It is predicted that Canary Wharf will be the World's leading financial centre. With this in mind British Telecom and Mercury Telecommunications have established satellite earth stations locally to handle highly advanced communication facilities.

The Isle of Dogs is at the heart of Docklands transformation and is currently the centre of development and the focus of commercial interest. Most of the area is covered by the Enterprise Zone which was established in 1982. Within this zone planning control has been relaxed. Furthermore there have been financial incentives: a 100% tax allowance for capital expenditure on new buildings and an exemption from non-domestic rates. These benefits, which have been of immense value to investors and occupiers alike, ended in April 1992.

Tradition and History

The Isle of Dogs lies at the centre of the East End. Its peninsula shape and river location give the area an unique atmosphere of tradition and history. The origin of the name is unclear. It is said that when Royalty occupied the Royal Palace at Greenwich, they exercised their hunting dogs on the island. The barking of these dogs was heard by sailors in passing ships, who gave the Isle its name. In the 18th century, the village of Millwall on the western side of the Isle of Dogs became well known for its rows of windmills - from whence the area takes its name.

The Island became famous at the beginning of the 19th century when the West India Docks were built. In the 1850s shipbuilding and engineering flourished and the Isle had thousands of migrant workers who came from all over the country to operate the docks and local industry. The prosperity continued for about twelve decades until the docks were closed about 1970. The area lay derelict until 1981 when the London Docklands Development Corporation was formed and has since transformed the Island through a series of major investment incentives.

Isle of Dogs from the west

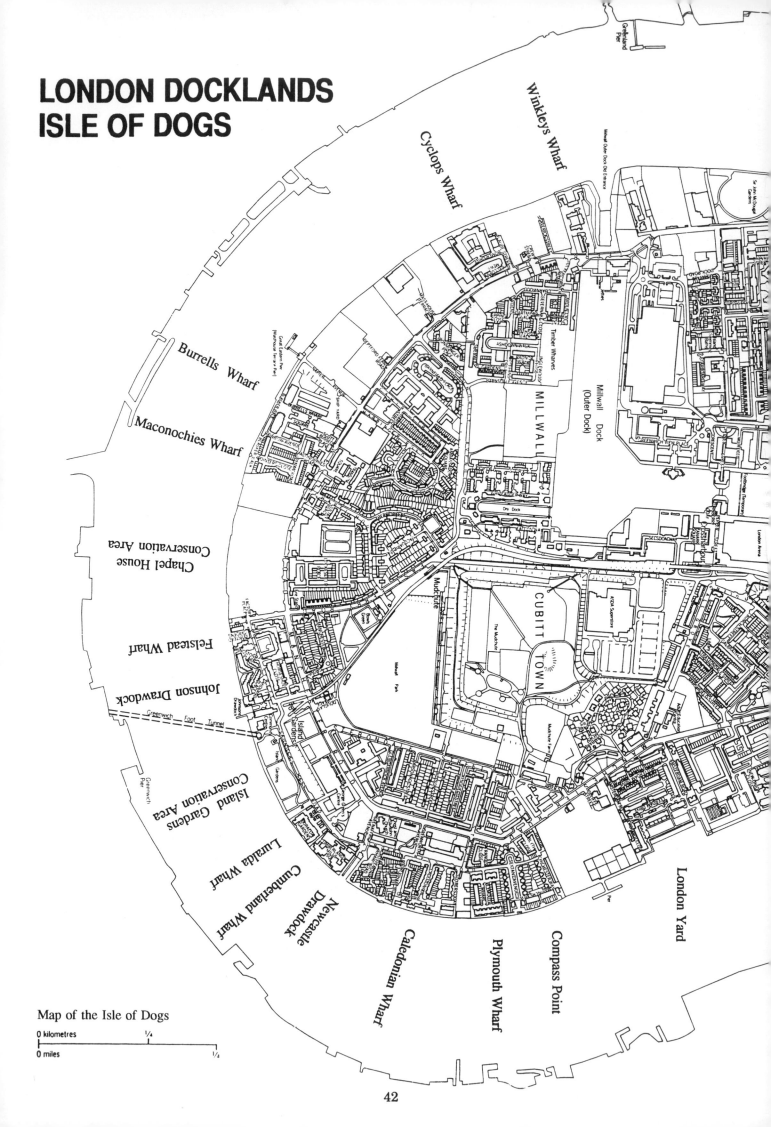

LONDON DOCKLANDS
ISLE OF DOGS

Greenland Pier

Winkleys Wharf

Cyclops Wharf

Millwall Outer Dock Old Entrance

Sir John McDougall Gardens

Burrells Wharf

Great Eastern Pier
(Masthouse Terrace Pier)

Maconochies Wharf

Timber Wharves

MILLWALL Dock
(Outer Dock)

London Arena

Dry Dock

Chapel House Conservation Area

Felstead Wharf

Millwall Park

CUBITT TOWN

The Mudchute

ASDA Superstore

Mudchute

Johnson Drawdock

Greenwich Foot Tunnel

Island Gardens

Greenwich Pier

Island Gardens Conservation Area

Luralda Wharf

Cumberland Wharf

Newcastle Drawdock

Pier

London Yard

Caledonian Wharf

Plymouth Wharf

Compass Point

Map of the Isle of Dogs

0 kilometres   ¼

0 miles   ¼

42

West India Docks
Conservation Area

Canary Wharf

Westferry Circus

Pumping Station

Cascade

The Anchorage

Seacon

Atlas Wharf

The Gun Pub

Coldharbour
Conservation Area

New
Pumping Station

Blackwall

Blackwall Yard

Reuters Building

Brunswick Wharf

Fin. Times

India

East

43

Redevelopments

The changes have been dramatic. Many hundreds of companies have moved their business into the area. Stylish housing and riverside complexes have sprung up all over the Isle. Thousands of people have set up home. The advantages are tremendous. The City and West End are a short ride by the Docklands Light Railway and express riverbus services are available. The Isle of Dogs has been injected with new life and new prosperity, yet much of its old character still remains.

Over the past few years a large number of projects have been completed on the Isle of Dogs. The Canary Wharf development Company has developed major buildings with retail and leisure facilities. There are two 400-bed hotels, 6500 car parking spaces and a series of interconnected landscaped courtyards, parks and plazas. Other office developments completed include South Quay Plaza, Harbour Exchange, City Harbour, Glengall Bridge, Scandinavian Centre, Thames Quay, Builders Centre, Greenwich View and Meridian Gate. One of the most important additions to sport and leisure in London is the London Arena that can convert at short notice to a 12,500 seat auditorium with the capacity to host international events.

The scale of development on the Isle of Dogs has been tremendous and has outpaced the initial provision of infrastructure and services. It is predicted that employment on the Island will rise to over 160,000 early next century. The main priority is therefore to improve road and rail links to meet these new demands. Construction of the Limehouse Link Road will be completed during 1993 together with other highway improvement schemes. The Dockland Light Railway eastern extension serving the Isle of Dogs and the Royal Docks will be opened at the end of 1992.

Arrive in the Isle of Dogs and you will find an area full of history and dramatic redevelopment, with a wealth of things to see and do. In the same day you could stretch your legs along a heritage trail in a conservation area with historic buildings, riverside pubs and old churches and later take a stroll along Marsh Wall on the Isle of Dogs and see the world's largest and most exciting commercial skyscrapers, which have taken shape on the Canary Wharf. The new commercial and residential developments are first described followed by a number of heritage trails of the historic sites on the Island.

Development along Millwall Inner and Outer Docks

44

LONDON DOCKLANDS
ISLE OF DOGS

LOCATION MAP FEATURE NUMBERS

The features described in this section of the book are numbered as listed below and the locations are shown by the corresponding numbers on the map overleaf.

1. Canary Wharf	53. Lockes Field	104. Arnhem Wharf	
2. Cannon Workshop	54. Island Square	105. Millwall Pierhead North	
3. Dockmaster's House	55. Felstead Wharf	106. Vanguard Engineering	
4. Hertsmere House	56. 30-38 Manchester Road	107. 192 Westferry Road	
5. Port East	57. Luralda Wharf	108. Masthouse Terrace	
6. Shed 35	58. Cumberland Mills	109. Great Eastern	
7. Littlejohn Frazer	59. Caledonian Wharf	110. Timber Wharves Phase 5	
8. Heron Quays	60. Plymouth Wharf	111. Mill Quay	
9. Island Quay	61. Compass Point	112. Clyde & Langbournes	
10. Arrowhead Quay	62. London Yard	113. Lockes Wharf	
11. Cascades	63. Friars Mead	114. 14-28 Manchester Road	
12. The Anchorage	64. Asda Superstore	115. Mudchute Station	
13. Lenanton's	65. City Harbour	116. Glenaffric Avenue	
14. Seacon	66. London Arena	117. Cubbitt Town Wharf	
15. British Telecom	67. Harbour Exchange Square	118. Pier Street Site	
16. Waterside	68. Harbour Island	119. Millwall Wharf	
17. Ensign House	69. Bristow Cairns Triangle	120. 385-391 Manchester Road	
18. Beaufort Court	70. The Pavilion	121. City Harbour Phases 3&4	
19. Waterside C	71. Limeharbour Court	122. Roffey Street	
20. South Quay Plaza	72. London Docklands Visitor	123. Ladkarn	
21. Grant & Partners	Centre	124. Dollar Bay	
22. Mowlem House	73. Skylines	125. Old Pumping Station Site	
23. Passmore	74. Thames Quay	126. Pierhead Site	
24. Mastmaker Court	75. Meridian Gate	127. Coldharbour	
25. Enterprise Business Park	76. The Innovation Centre	128. Jamestown Harbour D	
26. Guardian Newspapers	77. Neighbourhood Centre	129. Blackwall Entrance	
27. Indescon Court	78. Docklands Scout Project	130. Poplar Dock	
28. The Lanterns	79. Harbour Quay	131. Poplar Terminal	
29. Great Eastern House	80. Telscher Brothers	132. Naval Row	
30. Great Eastern Enterprise	81. Mercury Communications	133. Woolmore Street	
31. Advanced Textile Products	82. Wood Wharf Business Park	134. East India Dock Site C	
32. Northern & Shell	83. Cottons Landing Phase C	135. East India Dock Site E1	
33. Enterprise House	84. Cottons Landing	136. East India Dock Site F	
34. PDX	85. Yabsley Street	137. Brunswick Wharf	
35. Milltech Centre	86. Post 16 College	138. East India Dock Basin	
36. Glengall Bridge	87. Docklands Light Railway Depot	139. Garford Street Triangle	
37. Greenwich View	88. Poplar Business Park	140. Stoneyard Lane	
38. Westferry Printers	89. 216-242 Poplar High Street	141. West India House Car Park	
39. Glengall Place	90. 260-268 Poplar High Street	142. Yabsley Street	
40. Tiller Court	91. 272-286 Poplar High Street	143. Duthrie Street	
41. Atlas Wharf	92. Bazeley Street/Cotton Street	144. Ditchburn Street	
42. Docklands Sailing Centre	93. Financial Times	145. Poplar Fire Station	
43. Timber Wharves	94. East India Dock	146. East India Dock Site E2	
44. Winkleys Wharf	95. Reuters	147. East India Dock Site G	
45. Cyclops Wharf	96. Blackwall Yard	148. Blackwall Goods Yard	
46. Quay West	97. KDD Telehouse	149. Trinity Buoy Wharf	
47. Masthouse Terrace	98. Millwall Triangle Sites	150. The Limmo Site	
48. Burrell's Wharf	99. Arrowhead B	151. Thames Wharf	
49. Maconochies Wharf	100. Hutchings Wharf		
50. 411 Westferry Road	101. Empire Works		
51. Cahir Street	102. Ocean Wharf		
52. Clippers Quay	103. 223 Westferry Road		

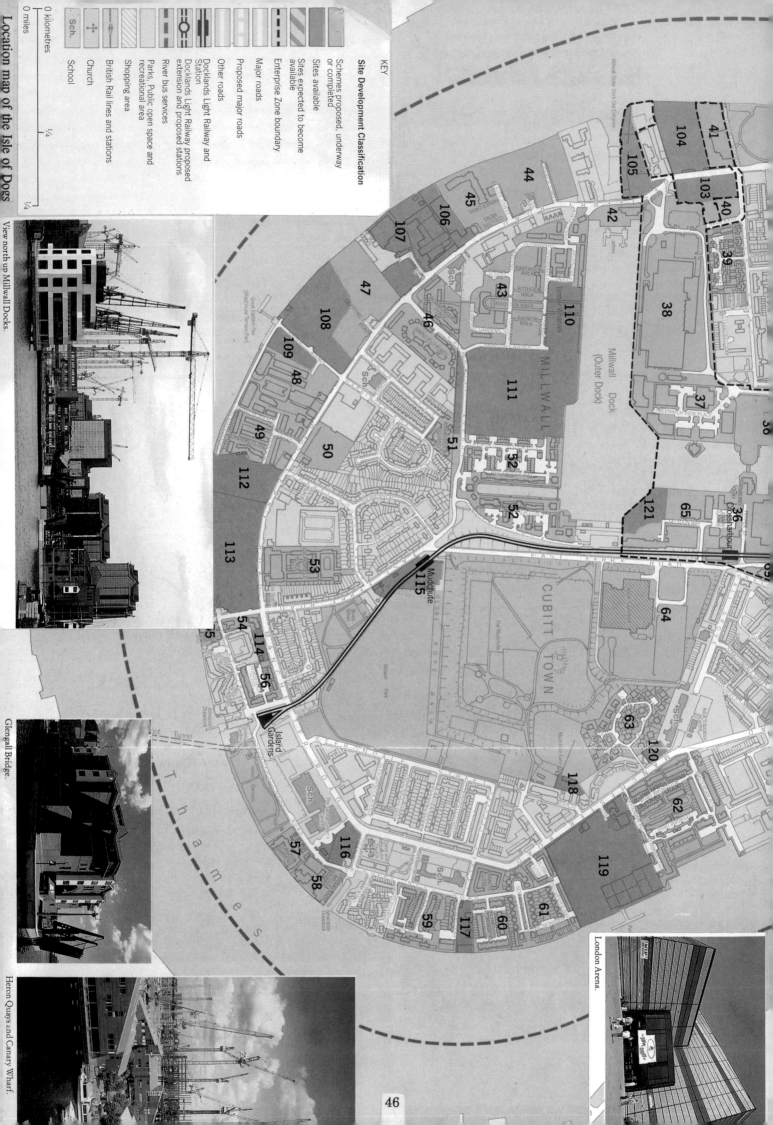

Location map of the Isle of Dogs

KEY

Site Development Classification

Schemes proposed, underway or completed

Sites expected to become available

Sites available

Enterprise Zone boundary

Major roads

Proposed major roads

Other roads

Docklands Light Railway and Station

Docklands Light Railway proposed extension and proposed stations

River bus services

Shopping area

Parks, Public open space and recreational area

British Rail lines and stations

School

Church

Sch. School

0 kilometres   ¼   ½   ¾
0 miles   ¼

View north up Millwall Docks.

Glengall Bridge.

Heron Quays and Canary Wharf.

London Arena.

MILLWALL

Millwall Dock (Outer Dock)

CUBITT TOWN

EAST FERRY ROAD

Island Gardens

Tunnel

T h a m e s

46

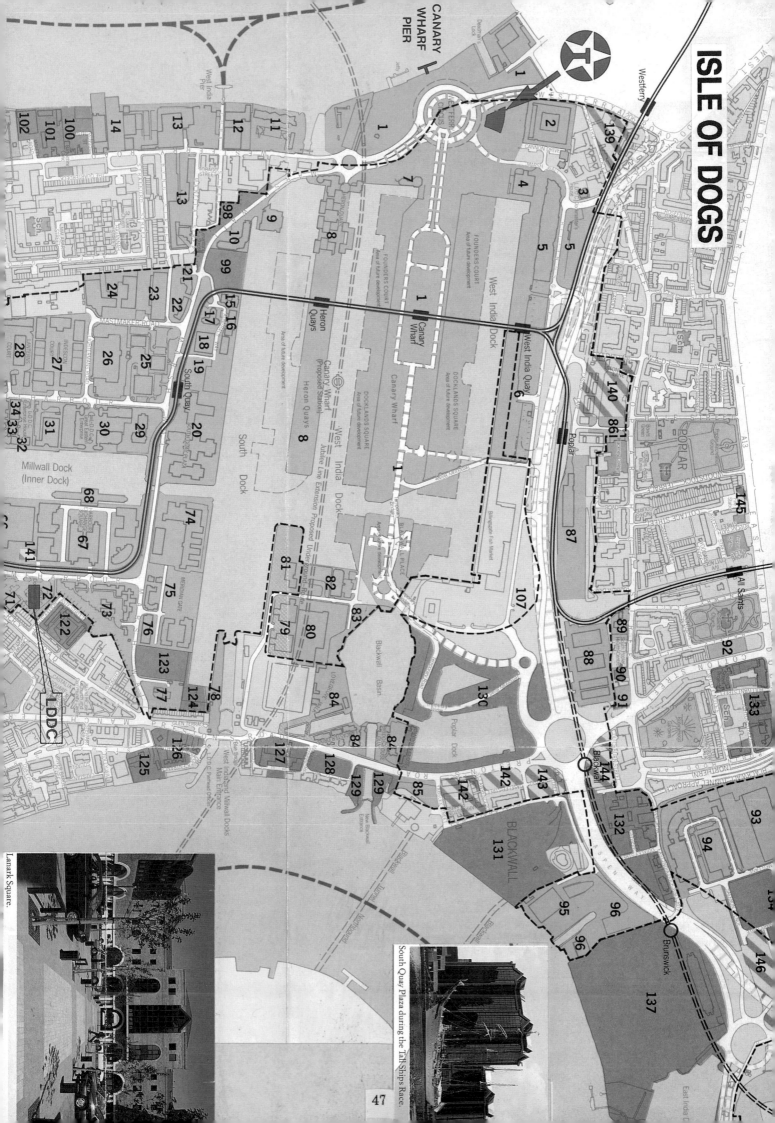

ISLE OF DOGS

CANARY WHARF PIER

Westferry

West India Pier

FOUNDERS COURT
Area of future development

West India Dock

DOCKLANDS SQUARE
Area of future development

Canary Wharf

Heron Quays

West India Quay

Poplar

Canary Wharf
(Proposed Station)

Heron Quays

South Quay

South Dock

West India Dock

Jubilee Line Extension
Proposed Underground Route

Area of future development

Millwall Dock
(Inner Dock)

Blackwall Basin

Poplar Dock

POPLAR

All Saints

LDDC

West India and Millwall Docks
Main Entrance

New Blackwall
Entrance

Blackwall

Brunswick

BLACKWALL

131

Lanark Square.

South Quay Plaza during the Tall Ships Race.

47

CANARY WHARF - THE JEWEL IN DOCKLANDS CROWN

Glorious History

Historically, the new Canary Wharf development is tied to London's proud mercantile past. On this site in 1806, the West India Docks were completed to become one of the wonders of the world at that time. They launched London as an international financial centre and dominated world trade for one and a half centuries. The system of wet docks with locks and spacious fairways ensured a secured shipping haven on an unprecedented scale. The quays were lined with monumental warehouses and a sophisticated system of cranes, winches, blocks and tackle which enabled the great clippers and ships of the world to trade and transact business more efficiently than ever before. In scale and efficiency, the Canary Wharf could be described as the West India Docks modern day equivalent.

In the 19th century, Canary Wharf was called the Rum Quay and was the home of the Mahogany Sheds and Rum Warehouses. Aromatic cargo from West Indian ships were stored in the warehouses and vaults and various coopering operations were carried out on behalf of the merchants concerned. The vaults were well built but not as extensive as those of London Docks. In 1936 the quayside caught fire and later was heavily bombed during the war. Post war the site was cleared and sheds Nos 10 and 11 were built. The Canary Wharf became a tenant berth for the Fred Olsen Line discharging Canary Islands' tomatoes and bananas. The Wharf had a distinctive smell of tomatoes on the quayside! The fruit traffic from east and west Mediterranean ports was quite heavy.

After the closure of the docks in 1970 Shed No 10 was leased to Limehouse Studios for film making but was demolished in 1986 to make way for the new giant Canary Wharf.

International Financial Centre

London Docklands' Canary Wharf is simply the world's most ambitious urban regeneration project and the biggest single civil engineering project undertaken anywhere. The scheme involves 26 office developments including one of the tallest skyscrapers in Europe and another tower block similar in scale to the City's National Westminster building. The construction price for regenerating this former wharf of the old West India Docks is £4,000 million. The Canary Wharf is bigger than the Channel Tunnel works. Most of the buildings on this 71 acre site are overlooking water and include a basement car park three storeys deep. The Canadian developers, Olympia & York, were determined to turn the Isle of Dogs into another commercial centre for London, similar to Wall Street in New York. [1]

The attractiveness of Docklands is very clear; so much empty space and so close to central London. It is very difficult to build office space for large users in the City because of planning restrictions due to thousands of listed buildings.

Canary Wharf Financial Centre

48

Canary Wharf looking north

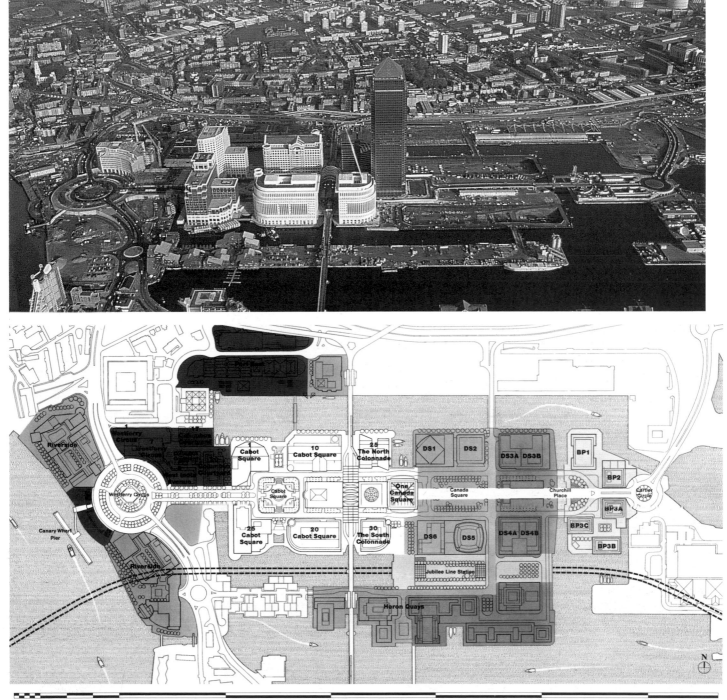

Map of Canary Wharf

Phasing	Riverside		Westferry Circus		Cabot Square		Canada Square		Churchill Place		Totals	
☐ Phase I	Total	1,090,000	Building		Building		Designation		Designation			
			1 Westferry Circus	230,000	1 Cabot Square	500,000	DS1	340,000	BP1	572,000	Canary Wharf	10,579,000
			7 Westferry Circus	160,000	10 Cabot Square	602,000	DS2	995,000	BP2	218,000		
■ Phase II			5 West India Avenue	133,000	25 The North Colonnade	348,000	DS3A	235,000	BP3A	144,000	Port East	550,000
			17 Columbus Courtyard	164,000	20 Cabot Square	532,000	DS3B	235,000	BP3B	104,000		
Phase III			20 Columbus Courtyard	169,000	25 Cabot Square	452,000	DS4A	218,000	BP3C	205,000		
			Total	856,000	30 The South Colonnade	275,000	DS4B	218,000	Total	1,243,000	Heron Quays	2,429,000
Phase IV					One Canada Square	1,242,000	DS5	901,000				
					Total	3,951,000	DS6	297,000				
☐ Phase V							Total	3,439,000			Grand Total	13,558,000
☐ Jubilee Line Station and Park												

All figures represent Net Lettable square feet. Information as at July 1991 and is subject to update.

The Canary Wharf is being established as a new financial centre in London to rival the City and the West End. The offices on Canary Wharf are spread around a boulevard and a series of traditional London squares with green open spaces. Pubs, restaurants and sport clubs are included at ground level with cars confined to basement carparks. The developers, Olympia & York, have imported methods used in the recently completed World Financial Centre at Manhattan in New York, the centre being about two thirds the size of Canary Wharf.

The Canary Wharf site extends over 1 km, almost the whole width of the Isle of Dogs from Limehouse Reach facing Tower Bridge to the west, and to the eastern side at Blackwall. The western end of the development includes eight buildings with a roundabout known as Westferry Circus. From there the site extends east along the wharf on the former West India Import and Export Docks. Most of the buildings straddle the dock walls and extend about 100m over the water leaving the land space for tree-lined squares.

Canary Wharf Buildings

During the early eighties, the derelict dock became a haven for wild birds and in 1987 this was topped with the arrival of the Canary project by Olympia & York. The total project comprises office space of over 1 million square metres including retail, restaurant and leisure facilities and a 400 bedroom hotel. A group of 30 to 50 storey towers overlook Canada Square. There is space for 6500 cars, the majority of which will be allocated to tenants, approximately one space per 170 square metres of net office space. There are new squares and open spaces and waterside arcades.

Canary Wharf has a total of twenty six separate buildings, including three high rise office blocks of considerable space. The opportunity therefore exists for large organisations to consolidate under one roof very close to the city. Apart from the tower at 50 floors - the UK's tallest building, - the other first phase buildings are mostly between 10 and 13 storeys with Credit Swiss Building being 20 floors.

In the first phase there are eight buildings including the tower. The lofty towers on Canary Wharf spread out far into the old docks on either side, and have upped the status of Docklands from a low rent industrial estate to a pseudo city centre. As currently planned, Heron Quay and Canary Wharf would be separated by a narrow 'canyon' in the waters of the former West India Export Dock. Both these developments fall within the Isle of Dogs Enterprise Zone which was created in 1982.

West India Avenue leading from Westferry Circus to Cabot Square and the Tower

Development within the enterprise zone is normally free of all planning constraints but is subject to approval by the London Docklands Development Corporation (LDDC) in three instances. First, if any nuisance such as a chemical plant were proposed it could be vetoed by the corporation. Secondly, any building over about 36m high has to be approved. Lastly, LDDC can stop development affecting sensitive subzones such as existing housing.

When completed in 1806 the West India Docks and warehouses were known throughout the world as its trade centre. In the twenty-first century, the buildings at Canary Wharf may become London's financial landmark recognized similarly throughout the world.

Westferry Circus and Cabot Square

One third of the site, approximately 25 acres, is dedicated to public open space. There are three major areas; Westferry Circus, Cabot Square and Canada Square, all complemented by a series of watercourts, terraces and promenades. Westferry Circus is a gently banked and mounded open area with gardens and promenades by the River Thames. Through traffic travels underneath the Circus. A new pier has been built to accommodate river traffic to and from Canary Wharf. The riverbus is owned by Olympia & York in association with the P & O.

The developers have created a "total environment" a whole new piece of a city. Westferry Circus is a large tree-ringed circus surrounded by buildings, with one segment open to the waterfront. It is the size of St. James Square and has been beautifully furnished with lamps, railings and benches. A tree-lined avenue leads into the first square, Cabot Square, which has an inner ring of trees around it and at the far side has a glass-roofed retail building full of shops, restaurants and beyond are the domes of Docklands Light Railway Stations and the giant 50 storey tower. The public garden is surrounded by silver lime trees and has the tallest fountain in London.

Cabot Square Buildings

Cabot Square and its eight buildings form the first phase of the project. The buildings and the tower block surround Cabot Square. The Credit Swiss building was completed at the end of 1990 after two years of construction work. Olympia & York is using much of the lower two floors for retail space and bank Credit Swiss First Boston occupies the next six floors. The rest of the building is being let.

The trees are one of the most important of all the elements which compose the landscape of the site and have created one of the best public spaces in London this century. The trees were selected in quantities and matured to a sufficient height to achieve complete and natural visual effect to improve the pedestrian spaces. The detailed horticultural landscaping has provided many thousands of flowers and shrubs.

Westferry Circus

London's Brightest Beacon

The Tower at No.1 Canada Square is the capital's most striking new building and is at the centre of a network of road, rail and water transport. The main entrance is on Canada Square, a broad tree-lined street entrances on the two Colonnades which border the building to the north and south. A short stroll towards the river lies Cabot Square.

Visible from all points of the compass around London, the 50 floor tower at Canary Wharf now dominates the skyline of the capital and marks the emergence of the brightest beacon in London. The tower is higher than the National Westminster headquarters in the City of London which has held the record for the past 14 years. With its pyramid shaped roof it is 245m high, second only in height in Europe to Germany's 256.5m high concrete giant skyscraper, the Messeturm at Frankfurt.

The foundations of the tower are supported by 222 piles, each 1.8 metre in diameter, reaching 20 metres below the level of the dock. On top of the piles is a reinforced concrete raft; nearly 4.5 metres thick which forms the slab base of the tower. The steelwork rises from the raft with an inner and outer structure to support each level. The exterior cladding panels, measuring approximately four by one metre, were lowered into position one at a time. During construction the outside surface was protected by a blue plastic skin which was removed as work moved higher up the tower.

The steel structure is designed to cater for the extreme wind forces that may be encountered and it allows the building to sway by as much as 300 mm (1ft). In the lower floors of the building, huge cross braced steel members weighing 33 tonnes transfer the upper floors through to the foundations. The steel shell and inner core are tied together with cross beams that support the decking for each level. The shell incorporates a total of some 28,000 tonnes of structural steel.

Much of the construction material used was delivered by barges from a holding depot at Tilbury and the transport operation was computer controlled. This was a revival of the barge traffic along the river. The steelwork was transported directly underground through a tunnel to the centre of the building for use.

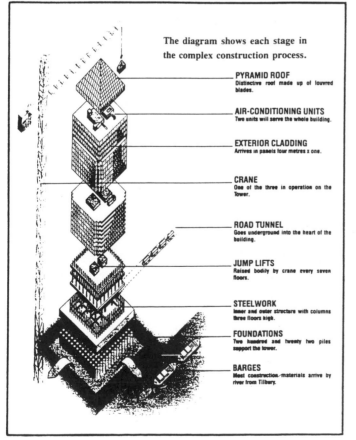

The diagram shows each stage in the complex construction process.

PYRAMID ROOF
Distinctive roof made up of louvred blades.

AIR-CONDITIONING UNITS
Two units will serve the whole building.

EXTERIOR CLADDING
Arrives in panels four metres x one.

CRANE
One of the three in operation on the Tower.

ROAD TUNNEL
Goes underground into the heart of the building.

JUMP LIFTS
Raised bodily by crane every seven floors.

STEELWORK
Inner and outer structure with columns three floors high.

FOUNDATIONS
Two hundred and twenty two piles support the tower.

BARGES
Most construction materials arrive by river from Tilbury.

The Tower taking shape

The Tower at No.1 Canada Square

There were three tall steel cranes which hoisted the steelwork and other materials into position. Two cranes were sited and tied inside the tower itself. The third was tied on the side of the tower on every sixth floor. As work progessed, the self-climbing cranes moved one step ahead. The final pyramid roof was placed by this crane. The roof is designed with distinctive stainless steel louvred blades, which are able to channel rainwater over the surface in such a way that the roof is self cleaning. The spectacular internal lighting makes the beacon visible at night across London.

On its completion at the beginning of 1991, the 245 metre tower became the tallest building in Britian. It provides 47 floors of offices and three floors of mechanical services. There are shops at the concourse level and below ground three floors for car parking, with services and loading access, and conecting to the main retail building and the water courts of Cabot Square. The attractive marble-lined lobby in the main entrance is two storeys high.

Future Building

Construction of the later phases of Canary Wharf has been postponed until the opening of the Jubilee Line Underground extension in 1995/96. The first phase of nearly half million square metres of office space has been completed and 90,000 square metres of phase two is underway. The only commitment for phase three is the 3,500 car park and a public park. Just over 60% of phase one has been let. Tenants were placed in the first half of 1991. By the beginning of the 21st century, the total lettable space of the whole Canary Wharf development will be over one and a quarter million square metres which includes the development of Port East and further buildings along Heron Quays.

Canary Wharf and Isle of Dogs from Greenwich

Canary Wharf buildings from the north west

53

PORT EAST AND HERTSMERE HOUSE

North Quay Redevelopment

At the entrance to the Isle of Dogs lies the North Quay which is part of the West India Docks Conservation Area and contains the famous historic Warehouses 1 and 2 and the Ledger Building. These will be described later under the chapters dealing with the heritage trails. In this section the new developments of the quayside are presented. West India Quay Station of Docklands Light Railway is at the centre of this area

Port East

Port East, on the West India North Quay and a short distance from Canary Wharf, is scheduled to open in 1993/94. It will offer an exciting mix of waterside entertainment and speciality shopping against the background of the historic Georgian Warehouses 1 and 2. Among the entertainment facilities will be a large semi-circular performance stage which will provide a forum for outdoor theatre and concerts. A multi-screen cinema, the largest in London, and relevant docklands museum will enhance the metropolitan atmosphere of the proposed development. There will be an international hotel and a wide spectrum of leisure attractions. [5]

Shed 35 Complex

Britain's biggest hotel complex is planned to be built on this site which is adjacent to Port East and overlooks the Canary Wharf. The 160m high building, six-star hotel, will be linked to a huge conference/exhibition centre. There will also be a 100m high office block. [6]

Billingsgate Fish Market

At the eastern end of the North Quay is the new Billingsgate Fish Market which moved from its historic building river in Upper Thames Street in 1982. The wholesale and retail fish market has two breakfast cafes and is open from about 5.00 am up to 8.00 am, Tuesdays up to Saturdays. There is a proposal to move the market down river.

Hertsmere House

Barclays Bank Building, Hertsmere House, is located near the gateway to the Isle of Dogs on the west side of the former West India Import Dock, and is adjacent to the Canary Wharf complex. In the old days, this was the site of the Port of London shed No 13 on Antwerp Quay which was used by the General Steam Navigation Company. [4]

The proposed Port East

HERON QUAYS AND SCANDINAVIAN CENTRE

Heron Quays

Heron Quays was the first major commercial development on the Isle of Dogs and lies at the foot of the Canary Wharf complex. Completed in 1986, it has a waterside business and residential community in the centre of the Enterprise Zone. The low rise Swedish-style buildings are surrounded on three sides by the waters of the old Export Dock and South Dock of the West India Docks. There is the benefit of its own station, Heron Quays of the Docklands Light Railway. A range of retail facilities including public houses and restaurants are available primarily around Heron Quays harbour, together with a marina and private moorings.

Heron Quay was previously the home of three dockside transit sheds, F, G and H, in the former West India Docks. The F shed was used by the Westcott and Lawrence Ships for export to the Middle East. The G shed was an important berth for the Ellerman Line and City Line for South African imports of canned fruit, wool, hides, copper, wines and spirits. The H shed was a mechanized export loading berth of Harrison Line and Union Castle to South African ports. [8]

Converted Barge Restaurants

On the Isle of Dogs there are a number of attractive converted barge restaurants. The Aak Salaam, a 1923 Dutch barge, is moored in Heron Quays. Leven Strijd, another Dutch Barge, is along Canary Wharf. On the South Quay, near Admiral's Way, is a third 1893 Dutch sailing barge.

Scandinavian Centre

Another Swedish-style office building which is standing on piles in the waters of South West India Dock between Heron Quays and South Quay. The four storey building completed in 1988 has a central naturally lit atrium for display and recreational purposes. [9]

Heron Quays and Canary Wharf

Heron Quays, Scandinavian Centre and the Cascades

WATERSIDE AND CASCADES

Waterside

Located on the South Quay between the Scandinavian Centre and South Quay Plaza, this complex enjoys waterside views and provides leisure facilities near DLR South Quay Station. The office accommodation consists of **Quay House** of three floors with flexible office accommodation, **Ensign House** of six floors providing 18 self-contained office suites and **Beaufort Court** of 48 luxury business apartments. It has a waterside Plaza with retail facilities and a 350-bedroom four-star hotel. In this corner of the quayside of the former West India South Dock used to be the Port of London K and L sheds, which had basements for the storage of dates and figs imported from the Gulf. [15]

South Quay

South Quay is an office development adjacent to Waterside and consists of three buildings, Dundonwalk House, Waterside House and South Quay Tower, arranged around a covered atrium featuring two levels of retail space, restaurants and wine bars. The top of the tower is similar in design to that of the Canary Wharf.

The Cascades

The first large riverside residential tower to have been built in Docklands is the Cascades. Its unique "cascading" silhouette dominates the river entrance to the Isle of Dogs. It is a twenty storey block with two penthouses on the top floor. The West India Riverbus Pier is close. It provides its international residents with panoramic views, westwards towards the City of London and eastwards towards Greenwich. Facing the building is the "City Pride" public house. [11]

The Anchorage

A prominent riverside residential complex adjacent to the Cascades which has been built on the site of the old Morton House, the soup and canned food factory. [12]

Blacksmith's Arms

Nearby and located along Westferry Road, this pub was built in 1820 on the west side of the Isle of Dogs. As well as a good ale house, it boasts a ghost "Fred Slater"! He was a former landlord who died in 1850.

City Pride Public House

Waterside and South Quay

56

SOUTH QUAY PLAZA AND GREAT EASTERN HOUSE

South Quay Plaza

The South Quay Plaza is one of the impressive office schemes along Marsh Wall with waterside settings, its own Docklands Light Railway station of South Quay and parking facilities. There are three entirely self-contained office blocks of seven, ten and thirteen floors. The development includes a large shopping plaza inside the tallest block with public house and restaurant facilities in the southern part of the site. South Quay Plaza was the first major office development to be started in the Enterprise Zone on the Isle of Dogs. [17]

In 1967 the Port of London Authority built, at a cost of £1 million, the 'M' shed on the same site to handle the flood of products from Japan and the Far East bought in mainly by the Ben Line Ships. Sadly, operations ceased in 1969 when the docks closed and the building was demolished in the early 1980s.

Millwall Triangle Complex

A mixed commercial and residential development including a hotel has been built on this site. [94]

Great Eastern House

A green office building, on ground and five upper floors, is located on the corner of Marsh Wall and Mill Harbour, overlooking the waters of Millwall Inner Dock. It is known as Great Eastern Enterprise named after the SS Great Eastern which was designed and built by the Victorian Engineer, Isambard Kingdom Brunel and was launched on the 31st January 1858 from the Isle of Dogs. [26]

Guardian Newspapers

The architectural form of this building, off Mill Harbour, is said to reflect a synthesis of the technical functions associated with newspaper press hall and paper handling. The slender tower evokes the Art Deco of the 1930s. [23]

Enterprise House and South Quay Plaza from Millwall Outer Dock

THAMES QUAY AND MERIDIAN GATE

Thames Quay

Thames Quay is an office building along Marsh Wall to the east of South Quay Plaza. Sitting on the corner of South Way and Millwall Cut, it is a brightly visible building with a design which is reminiscent of the form and detailing of an ocean ship. The terraces which ripple down the north and western elevations have pleasant waterside views with generous walkways open to the public. It is occupied by the London Docklands Development Corporation and by Norex, the Insurance Broking, Travel and Shipping group. In the 1950s a different kind of shipping took place on the quayside. There was the 'N' shed, a recognized loading berth for the Harrison Line vessels carrying machinery, electrical goods, steel and general cargo to Weston Newport and Windward Islands in the Caribbean sea. [74]

Fleet House

Fleet House is a five storey office building adjacent to Thames Quay along Marsh Wall. The elevations are clad in flamed and polished granite with attractive grey laminated glazing and a polished granite entrance hall.

Meridian Gate

Meridian Gate is a mixed commercial complex located on the waterfront of South Quay, adjacent to Fleet House. It consists of small business units with three headquarters-style office buildings with basement-level car parking. There is a plaza surrounded by shops and restaurants. [75]

Innovation Centre

The high technology Innovation Centre east of Meridian Gate has been designed to provide serviced units for research, product development, new technology and marketing. [76]

Isle of Dogs Neighbourhood Centre

Thames Quay and South Quay Plaza on each side of Millwall Cut

Harbour Quay

Facing Meridian Gate across the water and located on the North eastern quay of the South West India Dock, Harbour Quay provides two red-coloured self-contained office computer centres. Their entrance is along Preston Road adjacent to the Blue Bridge.   [79]

Dollar Bay

Dollar Bay is a commercial development of two office blocks with a car park sandwiched in between. The waterside buildings are on the site of the former Port of London Authority "O" Shed at the lower eastern end of the West India Docks. Note the old Stothart and Pitt cranes which have been preserved along the quayside.   [124]

Isle of Dogs Neighbourhood Centre

At the eastern end of Marsh Wall, this new building functions as a community centre for the London Borough of Tower Hamlets Neighbourhood Services.   [77]

New Water Pumping Station

This modern pumping station, located in Stewart Street on the eastern shore of the Isle of Dogs, regulates the storm water overflow into the Thames as part of Docklands drainage. The design of the building is said to reflect river flow at source and its natural surroundings. The large fan in the centre of the building's pediment is part of the ventilation system.

Meridian Gate water front

Developments along South West India Dock looking west from the entrance lock

HARBOUR EXCHANGE AND MILLWALL DOCK

Harbour Exchange

One of the largest and impressive office developments recently completed (1990) in London Docklands, Harbour Exchange houses a total of 100,000 square metres of self-contained offices in eight buildings of different sizes. The central plaza, surrounded by shops, restaurants and a pub, opens up onto a promenade fronting the old Millwall Inner Docks with its own water vistas. [67]

Millwall Dock Promenade

Harbour Exchange is located on the north east side of Millwall Dock within an attractive landscaped 4 hectares area. The retail shops, restaurants and a pub flank the walkways running into the central plaza. To complete the scene, a dockside promenade with conference centre and business apartments stretch out on piers overlooking the water activity of the established Albatross Club. [68]

The attractive setting of this development may be traced back to the old fine Millwall Eastern Granary which existed on this site and which attracted a large grain business from the Baltic States for over half a century. They were demolished in the late 1960s and replaced by modern sheds for the Fred Olsen Line. These were flattened in the early 1980s to make way for the present buildings. Two dockside cranes have been renovated and incorporated within the landscape of the new buildings.

Skylines

Skylines is a park of small self-contained office buildings designed for owner-occupation by professional and service organisations. It is located opposite Harbour Exchange at the junction of Limeharbour and Marshwall. [73]

Docklands Visitor Centre in Limeharbour.

Harbour Exchange buildings overlooking Millwall Inner Dock

LONDON ARENA AND VISITOR CENTRE

London Arena Sports Centre

Past the tall buildings of Harbour Exchange along Limeharbour Road is the London Arena Sports complex built on the site of the old Fred Olsen tomato and banana warehouses. Crossharbour Station of Docklands Light Railway is next to the building. The gleaming grey box type of a building, opened in 1989, has a main area big enough for a soccer match or the world's biggest indoor disco! It has a purpose-built exhibition and sports facilities with flexible performing space and auditorium, unique in Britain. By the use of hydraulically powered banks of seats, the seating capacities can be changed from a few hundred to twelve thousand within a short period. Crossharbour Station of the Dockland Light Railway links the Arena to Central London. Two balconies are capable of carrying indoor sprint tracks while the main concrete floor can be sprayed and frozen to form an ice-rink within a few hours. The absence of intermediate supporting pillars provides an unimpaired view for spectators from all corners of the arena. The Arena is the largest sport entertainment and leisure complex built in London since the establishment of Wembley Stadium over 50 years ago.   [66]

Docklands Visitor Centre

The London Docklands Development Corporation has a Visitor Centre at 3 Millharbour. It has an exhibition area and and provides information relating to developments in Docklands to the general public, schools and business people. There is also a Visitor Centre shop and a vending area. The office building faces the London Arena.   [72]

The Pavilion

The Pavilion is an office accommodation block to the south of the Visitor Centre with a typical city style architecture. The adjacent Limeharbour Court is of similar construction. [70]

The George Public House

Off Limeharbour in Glengall Grove, this friendly public house is a Grade 2 listed Victorian building of late 19th century construction.

London Arena overlooking Millwall Dock.

Limeharbour road on the east side of the Isle of Dogs showing Harbour Exchange

GLENGALL BRIDGE AND CITY HARBOUR

Glengall Bridge

The Glengall Bridge is a mixed commercial, retail and residential development completed in 1989. It spans the waters of Millwall Inner Dock with a new lifting Dutch-style steel bridge and lies north of the City Harbour and Greenwich View buildings. The East Quay comprises office buildings, business apartments, residential units and a restaurant/wine bar. The West Quay has similar composition of business suites and residential flats. Cross Harbour Station of Docklands Light Railway is to the east of the complex. [36]

In 1867 the Millwall Dock Company built a drawbridge which carried the Glengall Grove Road, over the inner dock at Millwall and connected the east and west sides of the Isle of Dogs. The knuckles of this old bridge restricted berthing and in 1963 a covered bridge with glass sides was constructed. The opening section of the bridge was provided by a single bascule which at night provided an illuminated landmark when the bridge was open. The second bridge was demolished in the early 1980s.

City Harbour

A waterfront scheme that combines office accommodation, hotel, restaurant, wine bar and a medical centre with an adjacent leisure and watersports centre to the south of Glengall Bridge. There are three office blocks A, B and C of 5, 7 and 8 floors with provision for small domestic scale office units. The 237 bedroom hotel is set in an attractive position overlooking the south-eastern end of Millwall Docks. Originally it was planned as a 30-storey building but had to be reduced to ten to match surrounding buildings. A health and fitness screening centre particularly aimed at medical care for athletes using the nearby Docklands Arena Sports Centre is provided. [65]

Asda Superstore

On the east side of Limeharbour and facing City Harbour is the Asda Superstore with a large car park, serving the Isle of Dogs and surrounding area. [64]

The west side of Glengall Bridge

City Harbour on the east side of Millwall Outer Dock.

GREENWICH VIEW AND TELEGRAPH PRINT WORKS

Greenwich View

Greenwich View is a development of offices and high-tech business suites with views across Millwall Outer Dock and the Thames to Greenwich. The scheme is in an attractive corner position fronting Millwall Outer Dock with the Daily Telegraph Print Works to the west and Glengall Bridge Development to the north. Two self-contained waterside office buildings on three floors are for computer installations. A spectacular island office building is constructed in the water of the dock. [37]

City Reach and Pointe North

City Reach the last phase of the development completed in 1990 is clad in silver-grey glass with contrasting detailing in polished granite and tinted glass spandrels. The spectacular reception area at ground level has marble on the atrium floor and mature trees in granite planters. Adjacent, but projecting further into the Dock, is Pointe North, one of Docklands individually designed buildings. There are balconies on two sides of the triangular building, and moorings are provided. The third building of nine floors is West Tower and is adjacent to City Reach.

Near this site was the old Millwall Central Granary which was opened in 1903 the first granary in the Port of London to deal with the Baltic trade. The ten storey building was 30m high and could hold up to 24,000 tons of grain in store. It was, sadly, demolished during the 1970s.

Daily Telegraph Print Works

To the west of Greenwich View and overlooking Millwall Dock, the spacious Daily Telegraph print works allows for an automated method of printing where the newspapers are produced in a process which runs in a straight line through the building. Along the water front, the original dock cranes have been left in place. [38]

Millwall Watersport Centre

The centre along Westferry Road spans the filled-in entrance lock of Millwall Outer Docks and has facilities for windsurfing, sailing, canoeing and water ski-ing activities. [42]

Daily Telegraph print works

Greenwich View facing Millwall Outer Dock

POPLAR AND EAST INDIA DOCKS

Cotton's Landing

These are waterside homes overlooking Blackwall Basin, the first non-tidal entrance basin for the old West India Docks. They are located just north of the Blue Bridge along Preston Road on the north east side of the Isle of Dogs. **[84]**

China Town

Agreement has been reached for the building of "China Town" on a 5 hectare site at Poplar Docks on the eastern side of the Isle of Dogs. The development will consist of a commercial, cultural, tourist and trade centre and will be carried out by the Mountleigh Group and the Tianjin and Municipal Government of the People's Republic of China. **[130]**

Reuters Building

A major office centre for Reuters has been built along the riverfront at Blackwall, the historic site of an old ship building industry. **[95]**

Financial Times Building

Further to the north in the Leamouth area, south of the A13, a large printing plant has been constructed for the Financial Times. The printing process can be observed clearly through its glass walls. **[93]**

East India Dock Complex

This development in the south west part of former East India Dock, has a mix of office, leisure and retail space with an underground car park. The four main buildings, three with atria, are at varying elevations and surrounded by a listed crescent-shaped, 5m high, brick dock wall, recalling the defended character of the former docks. The main buildings have white marble with bay windows and stone medallions. The scheme's relationship to water is emphasised by a series of canals and fountains. The complex adjoins the Financial Times building to the north. **[94]**

Cotton's Landing housing overlooking Blackwall Basin

The Financial Times print works

Naval Row Conservation Area and Hydraulic Pumping Station

To the south of the new development is an L-shaped conservation area bounded to the north by the old dock wall and enclosing parts of Naval Row and East India Dock Wall Road. At the eastern end and visible from Aspen Way is the former Hydraulic Pumping Station, built in 1857 for the East India Dock Company. The brick building is listed locally and has recently been restored. It is adjacent to the elevated track of the Docklands Light Railway extension to Beckton.

Brunswick Wharf

The red brick building was built in 1952-6 as a power station on the site of the old East India Export Dock, which was damaged during the Second World War. It was a landmark for forty years until it was closed recently and its tall twin towers were demolished in 1989. The buildings, visible from Aspen Way, are proposed for major commercial and residential developments.   [137]

Poplar Town Hall

The former Poplar Town Hall, Grade 2 listed, in Poplar High Street is a Victorian Gothic building of pleasing appearance and is detailed architecturally throughout. It is part of the London Borough of Tower Hamlet offices. Further along the same street is the Poplar Technical College building built in 1906 in Portland stone.

All Saints Church Conservation Area

The superb church of All Saints, along East India Dock Road in Poplar, was built around 1820 to the design of the architect Charles Hollis. It has a fine tower and spire with pleasant green surroundings. It is within easy reach of All Saints Station of Docklands Light Railway.

St. Matthia's Church Conservation Area

Nearby is St. Matthia's Church, considered to be the oldest building in Docklands. Built in 1654 as a chapel for the East India Dock Company it became a church in 1866 and was encased with stone to give it a medieval appearance. It is no longer used as a church.

East India Dock office complex

All Saints Church

65

ISLE OF DOGS RIVERFRONT

Waterfront Developments

For those visitors who have not ventured east of the Tower of London, it is well worth making a visit to the Isle of Dogs to witness the sheer scale of redevelopment and transformation that has taken place. Out has gone the image of the 1970s East London with rows of terraced houses and vast empty warehouses that have fallen into dereliction. In has come an astonishing upsurge of housing developments that now provide elegant homes for the upmarket buyers from the city with an incredible change of lifestyle for the old and new residents. Starting from the north west corner of the Isle, the visitor can discover a variety of waterfront developments described below, travelling along Westferry Road and Manchester Road. There is a frequent bus service around the Isle. DLR Island Gardens Station is a convenient point to start a visit to these developments.

Atlas Wharf

The development of apartments, penthouses and houses all overlook the River Thames on the west side of the Isle of Dogs. There are open public spaces adjoining a new riverside walk.   **[41]**

Winkley's and Timber Wharves

The houses and apartments of Timber Wharves have been built on the south west corner of Millwall Outer Dock, the site of old timber wharves. There are three lagoons within the estate. On the west side of this development is the pleasant riverside residential complex of Winkley's Wharf.   **[43]**

Cyclops Wharf

The apartments and mews houses have excellent views across the River Thames. There is a leisure complex on the ground and first floors of the main block rising nine storeys high.
[45]

Burrell's Wharf and Masthouse Terrace

Burrell's Wharf is a residential development on a historic site along Westferry Road on the south water front of the Isle of Dogs. There are restored listed buildings, warehouse style conversions and new apartment buildings surrounding the squares and cobbled streets of this riverside location. The estate is adjacent to Masthouse Terrace housing site.

Burrell's Wharf

Cyclops Wharf

Two centuries ago, Burrell's Wharf was pasture land, virtually unchanged since Roman times. In 1855 Mr. William Fairburn bought the site and built the first highly respected shipyard of its era. The first iron ship built on the Thames - the 164 feet "Sirius" - was built at Burrell's Wharf, and was followed by many others for other countries. But it was the "Great Eastern" which made the wharf famous. At 680 feet long and 58 feet high it was Brunel's masterpiece. It was undeniably a grand testament to Victorian engineering. Burrell's Wharf retained its shipyard for only a few decades and suffered decline as the results of lower labour costs of the northern shipyards. In 1888 the buildings were adapted to the production of dyes and paints which continued for almost a century.

At the centre of the development is the Victorian building The Plate House. Originally built to fabricate the steel plates for Brunel's ship the "Great Eastern" this historic building now contains a swimming pool and leisure facilities. Traditional Victorian architectural detailing has been retained and enhanced at the former gatehouse to Burrell's Wharf and provides office accomodation. The Gantry House and Mast House, both Grade 2 listed Victorian buildings, are complemented by the new facade of the Loft House, all of which contain business accomodation. Built around an unusual listed octagonal chimney, the Beacon contains warehouse style apartments. Distinctive double-height windows with exposed trusses are a special feature of the penthouses. The Wheelhouse and the Bridge are two riverside apartment buildings. Other buildings include the Quarters and the restored Forge with exposed internal brickwork, beams and feature ceilings. Mast House Terrace Pier of the Riverbus is near the development. [48]

Maconochies Wharf

Adjacent to Burrell's Wharf, the Maconochies Wharf is the largest self-built development in Britain. The houses vary in size and shape but they are all constructed of timber, white bricks and slated roof. [49]

Felstead Wharf

The design of this development is that of a Victorian warehouse building with steep roofs with a lantern and weather vane. The buildings have balustrading coloured in red and green. Dark stained timber and black steel simulate cargo hoists. It is near Johnson Draw Dock and DLR Island Gardens Station. [55]

Luralda Wharf

Luralda Wharf in a conservation area on the Isle of Dogs is a residential development built around a landscaped courtyard close to Island Gardens Station of Dockland Light Railway. They have large balconies with magnificent views of the River Thames to Greenwich Royal Observatory and Naval College on the south side. [57]

Felstead Wharf

67

Cumberland Mills

Cumberland Mills on the southern end of the Isle of Dogs is a waterside estate of apartments and penthouses featuring four pyramids with tiered roof top gardens. It is nearby to Island Gardens DLR station. It is alongside Newcastle Draw Dock where barges used to unload at low tide and where an oil seed mill flourished in the 1950s.　　　　　　　　　**[58]**

Caledonian Wharf

There are more than a 100 homes ranging from one bedroom flats to four bedroom riverside houses on the eastern front of the Isle of Dogs.　　　　　　　　　**[59]**

Plymouth Wharf

Adjacent to Caledonian Wharf, this large complex of residential units have excellent views of the River Thames to Gallions Reach and beyond.　　　　　　　　　**[60]**

Compass Point

Compass Point, the 100 homes complex, is on the south eastern river edge of the Isle of Dogs. Lying between Manchester Road and the River Thames, it has a range of styles from a classical London Regency crescent to the styles of Dutch architecture of gabled facades and bow-fronted bays.　　　　　　　　　**[61]**

London Yard

London Yard, along Manchester Road, is a Dutch style architectural development of apartments, penthouses and town houses on the east side of the Island. It has a large frontage on the River Thames. The estate is designed with varied roofscapes, featured gables and a central water garden with a canal bridge.　　　　　　　　　**[62]**

The Folly House

The Folly House is one of Docklands riverside restaurants situated in London Yard on the east side of the Isle of Dogs. The interior design is by Sir Edwin Lutyens, and the 19th century lined oak panels give the restaurant an authentic character.

London Yard and the east side of the Isle of Dogs

HERITAGE TRAILS ON THE ISLE OF DOGS

The Golden Era of Wet Docks

The West India Docks were the first and the most successful commercial wet docks built in London at the beginning of the nineteenth century. In their design and construction, they set a pattern which was followed in the other docks. With the complete redevelopment of the docks elsewhere, they are now the only survivors of the early intensive period of the dock. These docks pioneered a new concept of enclosed docks, with monumental multi-storey warehouses on the quays, within the security of a moat, boundary wall and a fence, all guarded by the Dock Constables. At the north-west corner of the Isle of Dogs there survives a unique collection and sample of the old features of an enclosed dock with its ledger building, guard house, constables cottages, excise and administrative offices, engineers' quadrangle building, workshops and stores, and two magnificent Warehouses 1 and 2. These buildings are the only surviving multi-storey brick buildings of their period. The two northern basins of the West India Docks were completed in 1802 and 1806 and were the first of a new era of dock construction with huge geometric basins and warehouses built for maximum efficiency. The Millwall inner and outer basins were built later in 1868 for bulky commodities such as grain and timber. Other historic areas include Coldharbour and Island Gardens on the eastern and southern ends of the Isle.

Warehouses 1 and 2 from Canary Wharf Tower

Listed Historic Buildings

The following remaining historic buildings and landmarks on the Isle have been protected by listing, some only locally, as the only tangible link with the Island's past.

West India Quay Conservation Area	Grade
Warehouses 1 and 2	1
Export Dock	1
Import Dock	1
Ledger Building	1
Dock Police Cottages	2
Gate Piers of Main Entrance	2
Salvation Army Hostel	2
Guard House	2
Quadrangle Building	2
St Paul's Church	2

Chapel House Conservation Area	
Docklands Settlement	
Railway Viaduct	2
Chapel House Estate	
Dockers' Cottages	

Island Gardens Conservation Area	
Ferry House Public House	2
Christ Church	2
Vicarage	2
Waterman's Arms Public House	2
Newcastle Draw Docks	2
Foot Tunnel Entrance	2

Coldharbour Conservation Area	
West India & Millwall Entrance Lock	2
The Gun Public House	2
Former Police Station	2
15 Coldharbour	2
Nelson House	2
Isle House	2
Bridge House	2

Poplar Docks and Blackwall Yard	
Hydraulic Pumping Station	
Blackwall Basin	1
Poplar Docks	2
Blackwall Yard	2

Walking tours may be planned to combine heritage and new development features. Examples could include the West India North Quay and Canary Wharf; Marsh Wall, Coldharbour and Poplar Docks; Chapel House, Island Gardens, new riverside housing and Maritime Museum in Greenwich.

WEST INDIA DOCKS CONSERVATION AREA

West India North Quay

This Conservation Area safeguards the few remaining historic buildings near the old main entrance gates of the old West India Docks complex. The nearest DLR Station is West India Quay. The existing offices and two warehouses are all that remain of massive brick warehouses along the North Quay. They are still very impressive when viewed through the old dock entrance. As well as the warehouses, there are a number of old buildings of great character around the main Dock entrance including three listed cottages in Garford Street, offices, guard house, police station and the quadrangle building which are worthy of a visit. There are the dock basins and also scattered around the dock area are a number of old buildings with some intrinsic character, such as the pumping station across the western entrance lock to the South Dock. Every effort must be made to retain or adapt these buildings as unique docklands heritage.

Dock Police Cottages

These three Georgian cottages in Garford Street with slated roofs are the last surviving buildings of their kinds and are Grade 2 listed. They were built in 1819 by John Rennie, the Engineer for the West India Dock Company, to house the police staff employed within the Dock Estate on the Isle of Dogs. The larger centre building housed the Sergeant and the two outside pairs for the constable ranks. The force was privately run by the Dock companies and the accommodation supplied was either free or at low rent. The cottages have been renovated and are now private residences.

Salvation Army Hostel

The Grade 2 listed building was designed in 1902 by Niven & Wigglesworth in the elegant 'Queen Anne' style surmounted by a cupola. It was opened by the Swedish Ambassador as the Sailors' Temperance House. The sea 'mission' was used by the crews of the various Scandinavian ships using the docks in the Port of London. In the 1930s the building was handed to the Salvation Army and since then it has been used as a hostel for men.

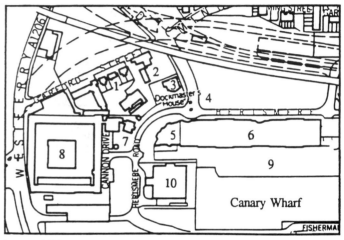

Map of West India Docks Conservation Area
1 Dock Police Cottages, 2 Salvation Army Hostel, 3 Dockmaster's House, 4 Gate Piers of Main Entrance, 5 Ledger Building, 6 Warehouses 1 and 2, 7 Round Guard House, 8 Cannon Workshops, 9 Import Dock, 10 Hertsmere House

West India Docks Conservation Area, the dockside sheds have now been demolished.

Dockmaster's House

At the entrance to the former West India Docks and adjacent to the Hostel, stands the Georgian Dockmaster's house designed in 1807 by Thomas Morris, the Engineer to the West India Dock Company. It was first used as an excise office, then became the Jamaica Tavern, reverting under the Port of London Authority to Dock Manager's office. During the 1980s the London Docklands Development Corporation renovated the building and sold it for office use.

Gate Piers of Main Entrance

The old West India Docks had a perimeter moat about 6.5m wide by over 2m deep. On the inside of this ditch there was a wall topped by cast iron railings forming the original security boundary of the docks. The Grade 2 listed gate piers dating to 1802 are part of this barrier.

The Ledger Building

Ledger Building

The Ledger Building on the North Quay of the Export Dock was designed by the architect George Gwilt in 1803. It was used as the General Office for the West India and Millwall Docks. All types of ledgers were kept relating to cargoes, including sugar, rum, timber, grain and general cargo. River tonnage dues and export documentation works were performed as well as the Central Wages and Cashiers. In the basement area, import documents and export files were stored. The large ledgers were locked up in a fire-proof safe housed within the Principal Clerk's office. All export and import general charges to merchants were dealt with by the Port of London Authority staff housed in the offices. The building was renovated in the early 1980s and was used by the London Docklands Development Corporation as administration offices.

Dockmaster's House at the entrance to the Isle of Dogs

Warehouses 1 and 2

Adjacent to the Ledger Building stands the last surviving group of magnificent Georgian warehouses from the early period of dock construction. They formed part of nine warehouses on the North Quay of the Import Dock, designed by George Gwilt as the Architect and William Jessop as the Engineer in 1800. The other seven warehouses were destroyed during the bombing of the second world war. Warehouse 1 was originally a low shed and was raised to its present height in 1827 by Sir John Rennie, to cope with the trade expansion of the West India Dock Company from the Far East. The warehouse was destroyed by fire in 1901 but the timber structure was subsequently restored. Warehouse 2, opened in 1802, had originally a timber frame interior but cast-iron stanchions were inserted by the Engineer John Rennie (Senior) in 1814 due to overloading. The windows were spiked framed to prevent intruders and the roof slated. The warehouses were linked through small openings at the boundary walls. The proposed redevelopment of the warehouses is called Port East.

Salvation Army Hostel

Quadrangle Building (Cannon Workshop)

This Grade 2 listed quadrangle building, now known as Cannon Workshop, was built by Sir John Rennie for the West India Dock in 1824. It has an imposing arched entrance of Portland Stone with granite door surround. The building provided offices, engineering workshops, stores and cooperage. Outside the engineer's office under the entrance arch is a cast iron plaque "THW 1800" indicating Trinity High Water level, the datum level of the Port of London. The quadrangle building was used by the Port of London Authority until the late 1970's when the docks were closed and has since been renovated and converted into units for rent by small businesses.

Round Guard House

Near the entrance to Cannon Workshops stands the Old Guard House, a Grade 2 listed small circular building designed by George Gwilt c1803. Originally one of a pair, one on each side of the entrance to the West India Docks, one building was used as an armoury and the other as a temporary lock-up for thieves. The roof dome is in brick covered with copper. The building has been renovated and used as a small office.

West India Import and Export Docks

The West India Docks complex consisted of the import and Export Docks, the entrance basins of Blackwall and Limehouse and the City Canal which was later enlarged to become the South Dock. They were completed in 1806 at a cost of £1.2 million. The locks and quay walls were designed by William Jessop, a distinguished civil engineer of his time. The two docks were originally connected to the River Thames for shipping via Blackwall Basin to the East and through Limehouse basin for barges and lighters to the West; the latter was later filled in. The new development of Canary Wharf overlooks both docks.

Western Entrance Lock and Pumping Station

Located along Marsh Wall between Heron Quays and South Quays, the lock was the western end of the City Canal built in 1804 to shorten the passage by about two miles around the Isle of Dogs. The disused entrance is the oldest to remain in London Docklands. The lock is blocked at mid length by an electric pumping station built in 1914 for impounding the docks water level. The outer chamber of the entrance lock remains practically intact.

Cannon Workshops

The north elevation of Warehouses 1 and 2

COLDHARBOUR CONSERVATION AREA

Coldharbour

This conservation area is about fifteen minutes walk from South Quay DLR Station, walking eastward along Marsh Wall to its junction with Preston Road, where the Blue Bridge is clearly visible. Coldharbour is a street of mainly 19th century houses built for the officials of the West India Dock Company. Lord Horatio Nelson is said to have stayed at No.3 Nelson House, while The Gun Public House in the same street, is reputed to have been his meeting place with Lady Emma Hamilton. The Gun was named after the opening of the West India Import Dock in 1802 when the first ship "The Henry Aldington" fired her guns as she hurled in through the Blackwall Basin on the north side of Coldharbour. The conservation area, on the east side of the Isle of Dogs, stretches between the two eastern entrance locks to the Blackwell Basin and the West India South Dock. The Gun Public House and the purpose-built former River Police Station form part of the fine river front. Some of the houses have been restored.

West India and Millwall Docks Eastern Entrance

This was the principal entrance lock for the West India and Millwall Docks. Originally opened in 1805 as part of the old City Canal, it was modified and enlarged in 1927. Power for the lock gate, cranes and capstans were supplied by the London Hydraulic Power Company. Today, there is a small modern hydraulic power plant sited on south side of the entrance to provide power for operating the local lock gates.

Blue Bridge, Preston Road

The large modern Dutch style bridge was built in 1969 by the Port of London Authority to replace the older swing-type bridge.

The Gun Public House

The riverside pub is in a corner position of the dock entrance. Its enclosed staircase has a peep-hole which was used by smugglers to watch out for the police! There is also reputedly a passage leading underground from nearby house through which Lady Hamilton used to get to the pub for her secret meetings with Nelson.

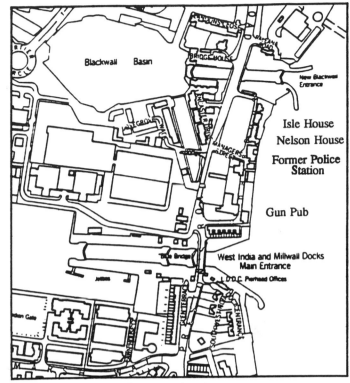
Map of Coldharbour Conservation Area

The Gun Public House in Coldharbour

Blue Bridge across West India Docks entrance lock

Former Police Station

The River Police operated from this building and all criminal matters pertaining to the river and docks were dealt with by a division based here. Police launches were moored alongside a jetty. The building has been converted into flats for private residence. A new block of flats has been built on the adjacent former Police yard.

Nelson House

Nelson House is adjacent to Isle House, dating back to the early part of the 19th century. For many years it housed the Dockmaster's senior staff but later converted into flats. The house is awaiting restoration.

Isle House

A grade 2 listed house fronting the river and is situated at the northern end of Coldharbour. It was designed by the Engineer, Sir John Rennie (Junior) to accommodate the Blackwall Dockmaster for the West India Dock Company. The building is awaiting restoration.

Bridge House

The Georgian grade 2 listed building was built in 1819 to the design of the Engineer John Rennie (Senior) to house the Superintendent of the West India Dock Company. Early this century, it became the residence of the Senior Dockmaster. In the late 1950s, the Dockmaster was rehoused and the building was converted into a training school for Police recruits. In 1990 the building was restored and converted into magnificent apartments and offices and is now occupied by the London Federation of Boys Clubs.

The Bridge House overlooking Blackwall Basin

Coldharbour with Nelson House and Isle House on the right

POPLAR DOCKS AND BLACKWALL YARD

Poplar Docks

Poplar Eastern Dock, just north of Coldharbour on the west side of Preston Road, was originally built as a regulating reservoir to maintain the water level in the West India Docks through a lock north of Blackwall Basin. Later in 1833 it was also used as a timber pond. In 1877 the Western Dock was constructed to become the destination of colliers carrying coal from Durham and the North East. The North London Railway established its depots here and operated the distribution. The areas are awaiting redevelopment as 'China Town'.

East India Dock Wall area

Hydraulic Pumping Station, Duthrie Street

The Pumping Station and Accumulator Tower are a few minutes walk from Poplar Docks at the corner of the roundabout of Preston Road and Aspen Way. They were built in 1882 to provide hydraulic power to operate the lock gates and cranes for the Midland Railway Yard and Dock. Constructed in red bricks with cast iron windows, it is typical of the stations built during the second half of the 19th century. The building is empty but under a protection order locally and awaiting redevelopment. [143]

Blackwall Yard

The site east of Blackwall Way, was an ancient place for River Thames shipbuilders and repairers since 1661. The eastern of the two listed dry docks appears on the 1803 plan of the East India Docks and is thought to be of late eighteenth century construction, partly rebuilt in the nineteenth century. Plans are in hand for the development of the site.

Hydraulic Pumping Station, Duthrie Street

Hydraulic Pumping Station, East India Dock Wall Road

One of the last surviving old hydraulic pumping stations in Docklands, it was built in 1857 and is Grade 2 listed. It provided hydraulic power for use in the former East India Docks and has recently been restored. [132]

Elevated track of the Docklands Light Railway eastern extension

Trinity Buoy Wharf and Lighthouse

Located at Blackwall to the west of the confluence of the River Lea with the Thames, Trinity Buoy Wharf was for 185 years the centre of Trinity House, the company responsible for operation and maintenance of all lighthouses around the UK coastline. The lighthouse and adjacent warehouse are the largest surviving Victorian buildings on the wharf. The lighthouse itself had no navigational function but was used for training of lighthouse keepers in the maintenance of lanterns. The beautiful octagonal lighthouse is unique and the only one in London. Built around 1860, it provides a link between the old Corporation of Trinity House and Michael Farady the inventor and founding father of modern electricity. During the Second World War the wharf suffered bomb damage resulting in considerable reconstruction from 1950 to 1963.

The London Docklands Development Corporation is currently using the east side of the area adjacent to the River Lea as a temporary Helipad, landing area for helicopters, but this use will lapse within two years. Some of the buildings are also let as artists' workshops on short-term leases. The 3 acre site is being marketed for redevelopment. The historic lighthouse and its warehouse must be protected. **[149]**

Trinity Buoy Wharf

CHAPEL HOUSE CONSERVATION AREA

Railway Viaduct in Millwall Park

This conservation area is bounded by the railway vaduct to the east and Cahir Street to the west at the southern end of the Isle of Dogs. Island Gardens DLR Station is nearby. The viaduct was built in 1872 and the railway service was known locally as the "penny puffer". The railway carried passengers and goods and was extended south from Millwall Dock to the terminus at now Island Gardens Station. The rail service closed in 1926 but it is now operating as part of the new Docklands Light Railway. During the air bombardment of the second world war, the sturdy arches of the viaduct were bricked and were fitted out with bunk type beds and used as bomb shelters.

Docklands Settlement

Built in East Ferry Road at its junction with Chapel House Street, in 1905, this establishment was used as a club for local women; also used as an eating room for young factory working girls. The building was purchased by the Docklands Settlement Movement in 1923 and became a popular boys/girls club.

Dockers' Cottages, Cahir Street

This housing consists of two terraced dwellings for workers' families accommodation and it is said that the cottages are the last dwellings of this type to survive on the island.

Chapel House Estate

The Chapel House Conservation Area has three estates of cottages built by Poplar Borough Council in the 1920s and 1930s. The Chapel Estate along East Ferry Road has red brick cottages in attractive surroundings.

Cottages in Chapel House Estate

Railway Viaduct in Millwall Park

Island Gardens

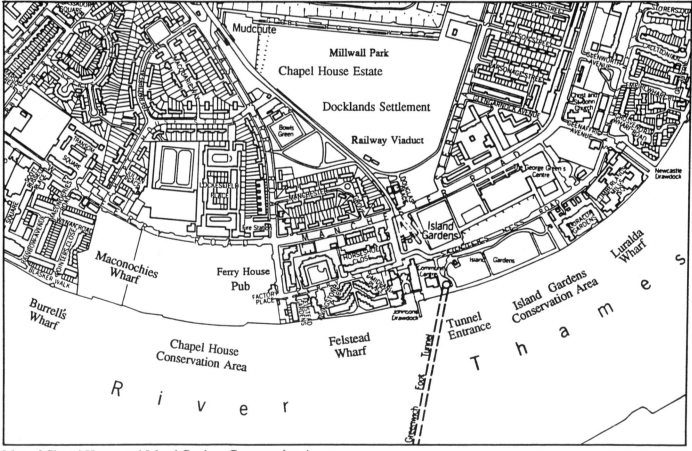

Map of Chapel House and Island Gardens Conservation Areas

ISLAND GARDENS CONSERVATION AREA

Island Gardens

This conservation is a riverside strip extending from Newcastle Drawdock to Johnson Drawdock and Ferry House in Ferry Street on the southern end of the Isle of Dogs. The gardens adjacent to Islands Gardens Station were laid in the 19th century by the Commissioners of Greenwich Naval Hospital. The gardens are fully mature and are well endowed with beautiful Plane trees. For its size, and because of its location, it is the finest park in Tower Hamlets. The entrance to the Foot Tunnel is located within the gardens. The Docklands Light Railway also terminates here.

Foot Tunnel

Opened in 1902, the tunnel replaced the ferry between the Isle of Dogs and Greenwich, and catered mainly for people working in the docks who lived in the Greenwich area and vice-versa. The numbers using it were so heavy before and after shifts that the two-way tide of human traffic always kept to the left. Nowadays walking under the water is a lonelier experience. It takes about 12 minutes including rides in the two lifts.

Ferry House

At the west end of Ferry Street is Ferry House Public House. At one time this was the only building on the southern end of the Isle of Dogs apart from the Chapel House. It linked in with the ferry and passengers from south of the river who would continue their journey up East Ferry Road. It is recorded that Pepys used this ferry in 1665. The Ferry House was rebuilt early in the nineteenth century. The inn has a tower from which a watch was kept in the old days for the ferry from Greenwich.

Historic Greenwich and the Cutty Sark

At the southern end of the Foot Tunnel is Greenwich which has one of the finest views in London. First to catch the eye is the Royal Naval College behind which is the Queen's House. The College was designed by Sir Christopher Wren in 1695 and has beautiful hall and chapel. The Royal observatory rests at the top of Greenwich Park hill. Greenwich is the spot where the international zero longitude is fixed, which is the Greenwich Mean Time. The National Maritime Museum contains the world's greatest maritime collection of boats, barges, paintings, ship models, weapons and naval uniforms.

Greenwich and the Cutty Sark

Greenwich from Island Gardens

On the waterfront rests the restored famous tea clipper Cutty Sark with her tall and graceful masts. Built in Dumbarton, Scotland, for the London shipowner, Captain John Willis, she was launched on the Clyde in 1869. The name dates back to 1790 and means a "short shirt".

Nearby rests another famous vessel, Gipsy Moth IV which came to Greenwich in 1968. The yacht, over 16 metres long, was sailed round the world by Sir Francis Chichester between August 1966 and May 1967 and covered a distance of 29,677 miles in 226 days.

Christ Church

Christ Church is an imposing Victorian building c1880, designed by Johnstone and built by William Cubitt. The high spire is a landmark locally.

Mudchute Park and Farm

Near to Island Gardens is the Mudchute Park. A new type of dredger for extracted silted mud was used in the 19th century for dredging operations at Millwall Dock. Thousands of tons of sediments were pumped out of the dock to form a 30 acre lake of soft mud, enclosed by banks of clinker, on the eastern side of East Ferry Road. In the 1900s, the dock company was sued by the local Poplar Borough. The council alleged that the mud dump was a serious health hazard. The mud dumping was stopped and the ground gradually hardened. During the first world war, the top of the mudchute was let out in allotments to local people. The island community campaigned successfully for the Park and urban Farm which it is today. The farm has housing for a variety of animals and serves as an educational centre for schools. The Mudchute Station (DLR) is a convenient stop for the park and farm.

Cubitt Town

To the north of the conservation area lie Cubitt Town and the Mudchute. In the 1840s, the builder William Cubitt leased some of this land for industrial development. Cubitt established timber wharves, saw-mills, cement factory, pottery and brickfields and built houses. The land leased by Cubitt was sold in 1955 and much of it was used by the London County Council and Poplar Borough Council for council housing.

Island History Trust

Near to Island Gardens and located in Manchester Road is the centre of the Island History Trust which came into being in 1980 as part of a community education project.It has collected many photographs of life and work and the artifacts which have allowed the Trust to produce a large collection of valuable and interesting archival material. The centre is well worth a visit and should have the full support of the public and industry.

Cutty Sark

Christ Church, Isle of Dogs

SOUTH BANK AND SURREY DOCKS

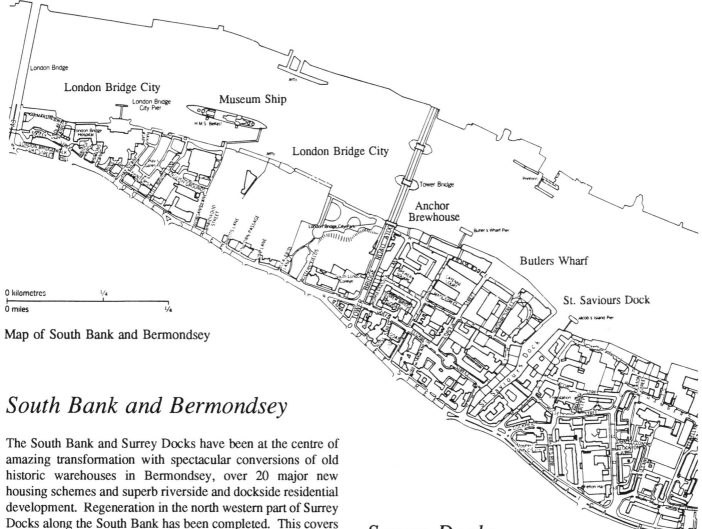

Map of South Bank and Bermondsey

South Bank and Bermondsey

The South Bank and Surrey Docks have been at the centre of amazing transformation with spectacular conversions of old historic warehouses in Bermondsey, over 20 major new housing schemes and superb riverside and dockside residential development. Regeneration in the north western part of Surrey Docks along the South Bank has been completed. This covers the riverbank from London Bridge to Bermondsey. The most important is London Bridge City stretching from London Bridge to Tower Bridge. The impressive development contains office blocks, a private hospital, housing and a leisure complex.

The regeneration of Tower Bridge Area, London's historic riverside, has also been completed and the beautiful Victorian warehouses around Tower Bridge have been restored. The old riverside warehouses downstream of Tower Bridge survived and remained largely unspoiled for over 100 years. This historic patch of London has been transformed into a fashionable district. All the listed buildings of architectural or historic merit have been retained and converted to new uses. The new buildings permitted have been largely designed in harmony with the character of Shad Thames and Bermondsey. The outstanding restoration and conversion of the old Courage Brewhouse, Butlers Wharf and New Concordia Wharf have created their own riverside character and is as much a place to live in as a place to work and relax.

Surrey Docks

The Surrey Docks occupy a peninsula south of the River Thames. Along the riverside most sites are privately owned and developed. In the interior the London Docklands Developments Corporation has substantial holdings which have been used to build mainly housing estates of many thousands homes. The major industrial development is the Associated Newspapers printing works for the Daily Mail and Evening Standard at Surrey Quays. The main links for public transport are the East London Line with stations at Rotherhithe and Surrey Quays and the riverbus has a number of piers.

The Surrey Docks have a thriving residential community with watersport in Greenland Dock and a yacht marina in South Dock and Nelson Dry Dock. Windsurfing, sailing, green open spaces, tree-lined walks and nature reserves combine readily with centuries old churches and riverside public houses. The riverbus runs regularly between Greenland Passage and Tower Pier for easy access to the City.

LONDON DOCKLANDS
SOUTH BANK AND SURREY DOCKS

Map of South Bank and Surrey Docks

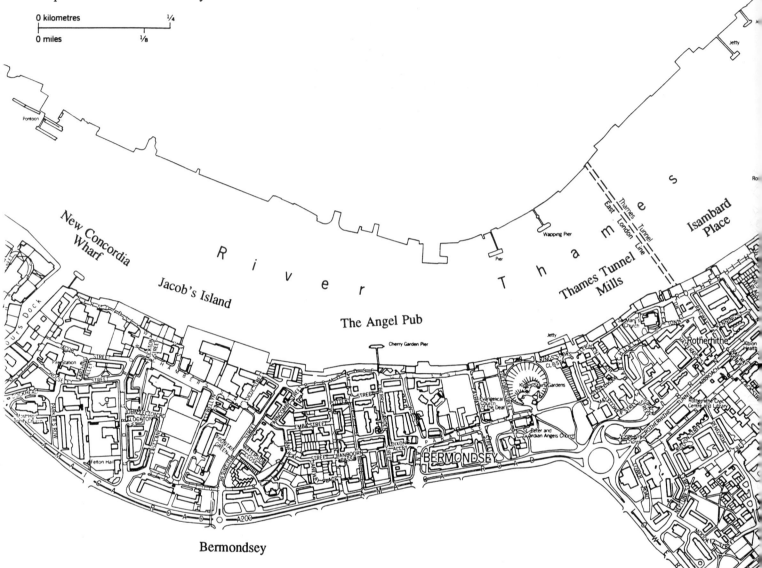

Bermondsey

Dock Office

Surrey Quays
Shopping Precinct

Rotherhithe

Rotherhithe at the top end of the Surrey Docks peninsula, is one of London's oldest riverside districts, rich in maritime legend and tradition. The Rotherhithe peninsula, once rather isolated and derelict following the closure of the docks, is now a flourishing community with its own new infrastructure and transport facilities. Some of London's best loved Thames-side public houses are situated in and around Rotherhithe. Walkers and nature-lovers are provided with wonderful open green areas like Lavender Pond, a man-made nature reserve where a wide variety of wild plants and animals thrive in just under one hectare of natural surroundings.

King & Queen
Wharf

Lavender Pond

Scandic Crown Hotel

Nelson Dock

Laurence Wharf

ROTHERHITHE

Stave
Hill

Surrey Docks Farm

DOWNTOWN

New Caledonia
Wharf

Greenland Passage

Entrance Lock

South Dock Marina

Surrey Quays
Station

Greenland Dock

Canada Water

LONDON DOCKLANDS SOUTH BANK AND SURREY DOCKS

Location Map of South Bank and Surrey Docks

KEY

Site Development Classification

Schemes proposed, underway or completed

Sites available

Sites expected to become available

Surrey Quays Centre

Major roads

Proposed major roads

Other roads

River bus services

Parks, Public open space and recreational area

Shopping area

British Rail lines and stations

London Underground stations existing; proposed

Church

Sch.   School

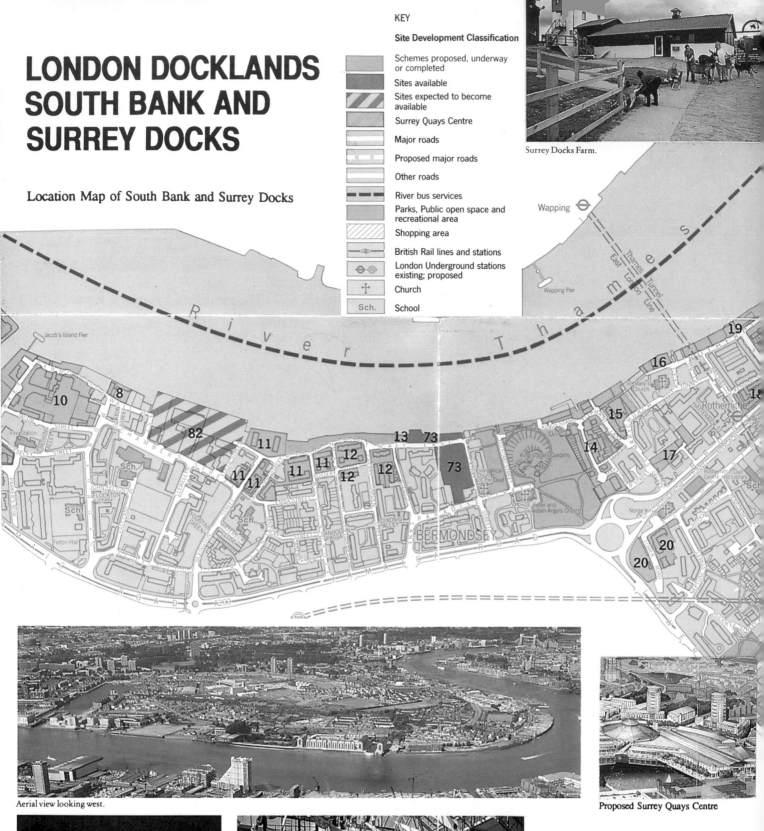

Surrey Docks Farm.

Aerial view looking west.

Proposed Surrey Quays Centre

Albion Channel, Surrey Quays.

Surrey Quays Shopping Centre.

Greenland Passage.

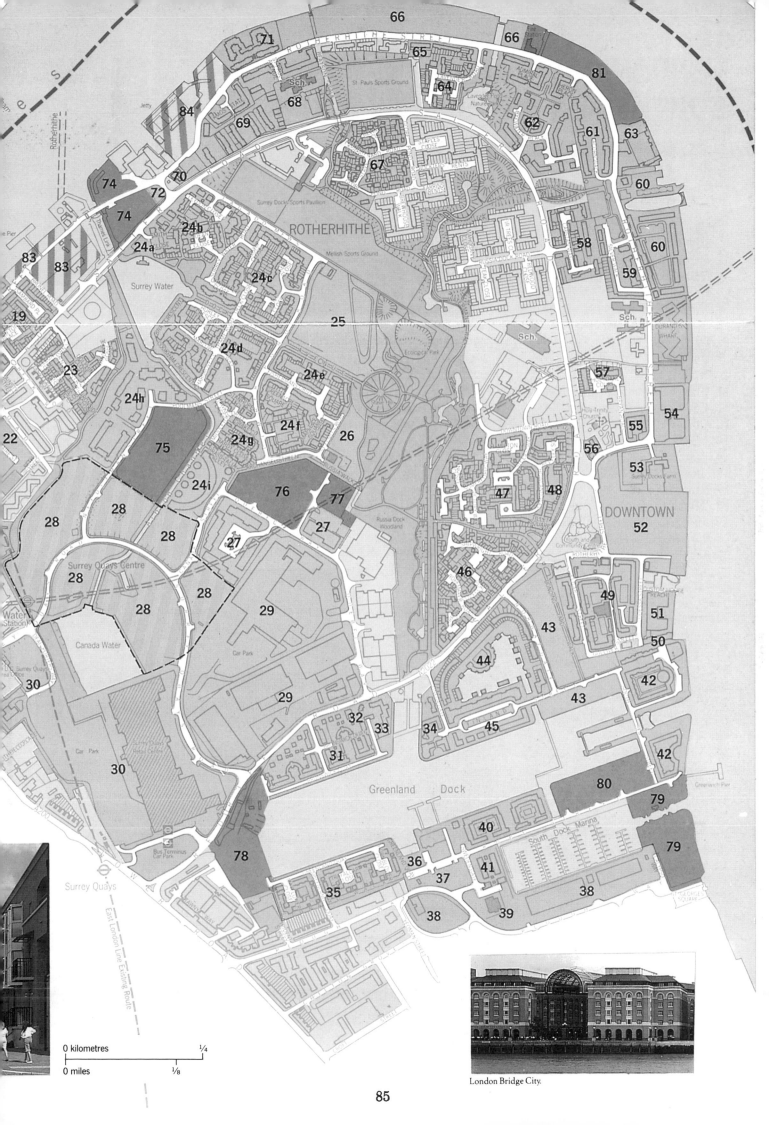

London Bridge City.

LONDON DOCKLANDS
SOUTH BANK AND SURREY DOCKS

LOCATION MAP FEATURE NUMBERS

The features described in this section of the book are numbered as listed below and the locations are shown by the corresponding numbers on the map on previous page.

1. London Bridge City
2. Tower Bridge Road
3. Anchor Brewhouse
4. Horselydown Square
5. Butler's Wharf
6. The Circle
7. Christians and Java Wharves
8. St. Saviour's Dock
9. Dockhead
10. Jacob's Island
11. Cherry Garden Pier (LB Southwark)
12. Cherry Garden Pier
13. Corbett's Wharf
14. Mayflower Court
15. East India Wharf
16. Thames Tunnel Mills
17. Rupack Street
18. British Legion
19. Isambard Place
20. City Business Centre
21. Renforth Pumping Station
22. Albion Street
23. Atlas Reach
24. Surrey Quays
24a. Abbeyfield
24b. Gullivers Place
24c. Stave Yard
24d. Marlow Landings
24e. Stave Hill Park
24f. Baltic Court
24g. Trinity Lock
24h. Hythe Point
24i. Wolfe Crescent
25. Bacon's City College
26. Surrey Quays Primary School
27. Industrial Developments
28. Surrey Quays Centre
29. Associated News
30. Surrey Quays Shopping Precinct
31. Brunswick Quay
32. Canada, Atlanta & Brunswick House
33. Russia Court West
34. Russia Court East
35. Greenland Quay
36. Watersports Centre
37. Tavern Quay
38. Marine Wharf
39. Mulberry Quay
40. Swedish Quay
41. Baltic Quay
42. Greenland Passage

43. Norway Yard/Finland Quay East
44. Norway Dock
45. Finland Quay West
46. Lady Dock
47. Reveley Lock
48. Nelsons Reach
49. Redriff Estate
50. Lower Odessa Wharf
51. New Caledonian Wharf
52. Barnardo Wharf
53. Surrey Docks Farm
54. Trinity Business Centre
55. Bryan House
56. Church House
57. Holyoake House
58. Acorn Yard
59. Silver Walk
60. Nelson Dock/Columbia Wharf/Laurence Wharf
61. Acorn Wharf
62. Lavender Dock East
63. Canada Wharf

64. Lavender Dock North
65. Rotherhithe Street
66. Lavender Wharf
67. Lavender Green
68. New Primary School
69. Amos Estate
70. Surrey House
71. Globe Wharf/King and Queen Wharf
72. Surrey House
73. Archaeological Site
74. Island Yard
75. Surrey Quays Housing Site 10
76. Surrey Quays Industrial Site C
77. Surrey Quays Industrial Site A2
78. Howland Quay
79. St. George's Wharf
80. Rainbow Quay
81. Lavender Dock East - Riverside
82. Chamber's Wharf
83. Clarence Wharf
84. Bellamy's Wharf

Surrey Docks looking west

LONDON BRIDGE CITY

South Bank Redevelopment

Regeneration along the South Bank was completed in 1989. The South Bank covers the riverbank from London Bridge to Bermondsey which used to be the western part of the Surrey Docks. The most important development is the London Bridge City, near London Bridge Station. An impressive mixed development which comprises offices, shops, apartments, a beautiful galleria and a new Park, including a riverside walkway from London Bridge to Tower Bridge.

No.1 London Bridge

Adjacent to the modern London Bridge and conceived as the gateway to the whole development, this office building has twin towers of 9 and 12 storeys which are clad in a subtle combination of flamed and polished granite and are linked by a spectacular atrium. The southern approach of the Old London Bridge (1831) crossed this site. The bridge was demolished in 1973, sold and rebuilt in the USA.   [1]

St Olaf's House

The Grade 2 listed building, built in 1931, was formerly the headquarters of Hays Wharf Company. It has been renovated and is regarded as one of the fine examples of "art deco" architecture in the country.

London Bridge Hospital

This prestigious private hospital was constructed within the restored facades of the fine Grade 2 listed Victorian warehouse of Chamberlains Wharf of early 1860s. Post 1940, the old wharf was a major warehouse for storage and distribution of supplies for American Forces stationed in the UK. The building is linked by a footbridge to Emblem House, also listed, which provides consulting rooms and support facilities for the hospital.

Cotton's Building

As the centre piece of the development, this new seven storey building is designed around an impressive central atrium through the glass wall of which is a spectacular view of the City and the North Bank of the river. The atrium contains an impressive sculpture and a cascade water feature with tropical planting. The office block, adjacent to Hays Galleria, has a basement car park and at the lower level a sport and leisure centre and a number of retail shops. Cotton's Wharf, originally built 1857, operated along this stretch of the river for over a century.

London Bridge Hospital and St Olaf's House

London Bridge City

HMS Belfast Museum Ship

This 1938 built warship, moored in the Thames off London Bridge City, took part in World War 2, and is now open daily as a floating naval museum. At 11,500 tonnes, the ship was the largest cruiser ever built for the Royal Navy and became famous for the part it played in the Battle of North Cape and D-Day. It is the first warship since HMS Victory to be preserved for the nation. The six decks of the ship are full of naval objects including uniforms and firearms.

London Dungeon Museum

The nearby museum of London Dungeon in Tooley Street has a gruesome collection of exhibits from British history. It illustrates horrors such as tortures, executions and murders in life size tableaux.

Southwark Cathedral

Immediately to the west of London Bridge is Southwark Cathedral, one of the best Gothic Churches in London and with some parts dating back to Norman times. It has a chapel commemorating John Harvard who founded the first university in the USA.

Kathleen and May Schooner Museum

Kathleen and May is the last remaining wooden three-masted topsail schooner. It is moored in St. Mary Overy Dock next to Southwark Cathedral. On board, an audio-visual display tells the story of the vessel and an exhibition shows the type of cargoes carried.

London Bridge City looking south

Kathleen and May Schooner

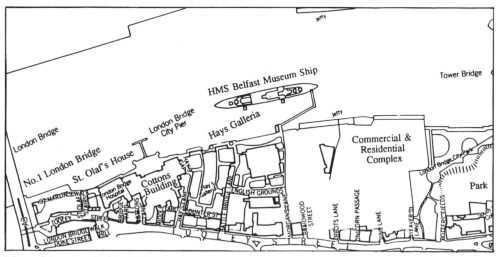
Map of London Bridge City

HAYS GALLERIA CONSERVATION AREA

Hays Galleria

An exciting reconstruction in London Bridge City that lies behind the attractive brick facades of the 19th century Grade 2 listed warehouses of Hays Dock. Hays Galleria was formerly Hays Wharf of 1857 where cargo ships from all over the world used to discharge. Its dock, where tea clippers once moored, has a magnificent glass roof 30 metres high, which is of Victorian arcade inspired design, while the charm of the old Victorian warehouses has been retained to form one of London's unique riverside shopping and eating precincts. The "Navigators" huge moving sculpture has water jets, fountains and giant bronze fishes and is a dynamic reminder of the spirit of the Thames. At the rear of the dock there were the grand tea auction rooms which now form the roof of a two level car park, inside the drained dock. The original cellars of the wharf with exposed brick vaults have been converted into a wine bar and shops. Hays Galleria may be entered either from Tooley Street or the Riverside Walkway. London Dungeon and Southwark Cathedral are nearby. London Bridge is the nearest station. [1]

Tooley Street Centre

This group of Grade 2 listed buildings of early 1900s, houses the Building Management Computer system which monitors and controls the services throughout the whole development. The Centre also provides residential accommodation for the management staff.

Riverside Walkway

This stretches the length of the development between London Bridge and Tower Bridge and has opened up the river bank to the public for the first time in at least two centuries. In front of the Cottons Building there is a grand setting for the Riverbus pier. A pedestrian bridge links from the low level walkway at Cottons Centre across Tooley Street to provide undercover access to the platforms at London Bridge Station.

The Horniman Public House

This is a beautiful new waterfront public house and restaurant of Hay's Galleria which has been most lavishly fitted. Part of the conversion of the historic Hay's Dock, the elaborate interior is based on the life of the 19th century tea shipper and traveller, Frederick John Horniman. It includes a gallery level restaurant with views over Tower Bridge and the museum ship HMS Belfast, and a cafe.

The Horniman Public House

Hays Galleria in London Bridge City

TOWER BRIDGE CONSERVATION AREA

Tower Bridge Conservation Area

This 'outstanding' conservation area in Bermondsey extends from the southern approach to Tower Bridge eastwood along the river to Shad Thames and contains some of Docklands finest examples of Victorian architecture. It includes the former Courage Brewery and the largest group of warehouses of the Butler's Wharf Company. St. Olaf's College buildings along Tooley Street and other warehouses are further preserved parts of the area.

Tower Bridge and Museum

Tower Bridge is one of the most famous bridges in the world. It was built during 1886-1894 in Gothic style to blend with the nearby historic buildings of Tower of London. The stonework conceals a semi-suspended steel framework and has no structural function. The engineer for the work was Sir John Wolfe-Barry and the architect was Sir Horace Jones. Jones died in 1887, whereupon the architectural detailing was taken over by Stevenson. The bridge bascules were raised by hydraulic power, the engines being housed in the bases of the piers, while power was supplied from a pumping station on the south side. Hydraulic lifts in the towers give access to the overhead walkway which is now open to the public as a tourist attraction. The old pumping station building is used as a small museum and bookshop for the bridge.

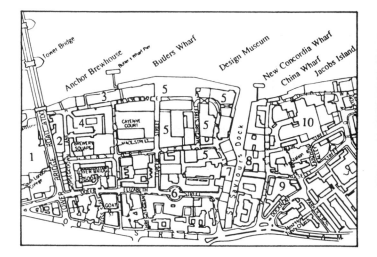

Map of Tower Bridge and St Saviour's Dock Conservation Areas. 1 London Bridge City 2 Tower Bridge Road 3 Anchor Brewhouse 4 Horselydown Square 5 Butlers Wharf 6 The Circle 7 Christians and Java Wharves 8 St Saviour's Dock 9 Dockhead 10 Jacob's Island

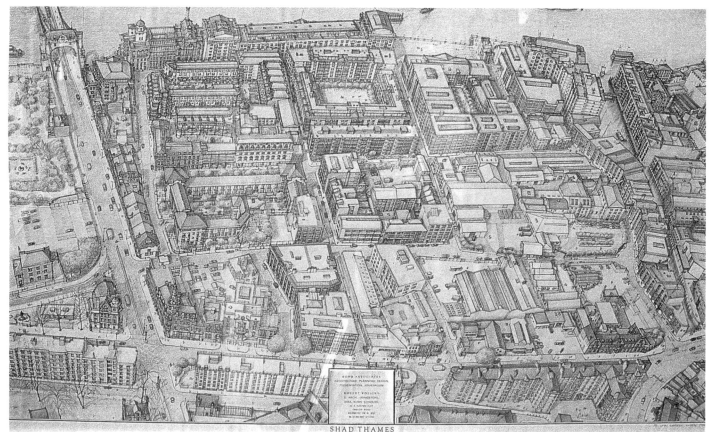

Artist's impression of Tower Bridge and St. Saviour's Dock Conservation Areas

THE ANCHOR BREWHOUSE CONSERVATION AREA

Shad Thames

This is one of the historic areas of London just downstream of Tower Bridge where a beautiful group of riverside Victorian warehouses have been restored. The maze of narrow streets with their distinctive tall buildings linked by bridges and walkways and forming 'canyons', have been the setting for many period films and dramas. Anchor Brewhouse is the first of these interesting conversions.

Anchor Brewhouse

The Anchor Brewhouse adjoins Tower Bridge and rises ten storeys from the waters of the River Thames. With its fine Victorian architecture and character, the historic building is a recognisable landmark from the north bank and has beautiful views of the city. A totally new interior has been created within the listed shell to provide apartments, most with commanding views of the River. The standard of refurbishment of the external features has been treated imaginatively. The restoration was completed in two phases, the first being a new construction erected within the shell walls of the old Boilerhouse. This phase provided flats and studios, all crowned by a superb three level penthouse. The second phase, known as the Malt Mill, provided further apartments with river views. [3]

Courage Brewery

The Anchor Brewhouse, formerly part of Courage Breweries, is a Grade 2 listed building and is situated in the Tower Bridge conservation area. Courage's connection with the building dates back two centuries to December 1787, when the Aberdonian, John Courage, bought a small brewhouse on the site. A year later the first entry in the brewing book recorded that John Courage had brewed fifty one barrels of beer at The Anchor Brewhouse, Horselydown.

The Malt Mill and Boilerhouse

Three separate elements of the buildings each expressing the different functions in the process of beer making, modified and altered over the years, are integrated to form the picturesque composition of this development. The form of the building clearly derives from its earlier function as a brewhouse. Though the upper part of the Brewhouse was destroyed by fire in 1895, the exterior outline of the buildings is largely unchanged over the past one hundred years, and their design still remains very closely related to the functions for which they were intended. At the eastern end lies the Boilerhouse with the tall chimney, in the centre of the Brewhouse itself, once containing the enormous copper brewing vats; and adjoining Tower Bridge, the Malt Mill, where in the old days, sacks of malt were hoisted from barges reverted in the River. The Anchor Brewhouse is considered one of the finest examples of restoration of its kind along the Thames.

Anchor Brewhouse adjacent to Tower Bridge

BUTLERS WHARF CONSERVATION AREA

Butlers Wharf

The Victorian warehouses of Butlers Wharf at Shad Thames Bermondsey, built 1871-3, have been beautifully converted into residential apartments with shops, museums and an hotel to create a 14-acre riverside community by Tower Bridge. Cinnamon Wharf, the first of the residential rebuilding completed within Butlers Wharf, comprises luxury apartments with views over the waters of St Saviour's Dock. Further north where the river meets St. Saviour's Dock the former wharf building, has been converted into a hotel. The restoration and conversion of London's largest group of Victorian warehouses and wharves were carried out by a consortium headed by Sir Terence Conran. The project creating over a hundred thousand square metres of accommodation in a five hectare site, provide luxury flats, studios, workshops, shops, offices and a conference centre, with pedestrianised streets and a riverside walkway. [5]

Old Tea Warehouses

The first mention of a Mr. Butler on the site has been found in the General Rates book of 1794 when he was in partnership with a Mr. Holland. They leased a group of warehouses at the north end of the property adjacent to St. Saviours Dock from the Abdy family who owned the site. One commodity they dealt with was grain. In 1808 Mr. Butler was operating a Wharfingers Company in nearby Tooley Street. In May 1872, Butlers Wharf Company was registered under the Chairmanship of Mr. Hutchins. According to records, the wharf became famous for handling tea. The Company grew rapidly and by 1945 it had three subsidiary companies one of

which, dealing in spices, is still in existence. In the 1950s the company was handling 6,000 chests of tea a day as well as coffee, cocoa, cassia, pimento, canned salmon and meats, drugs, pepper, nutmegs, wines and spirits. The ships of the General Steam Navigation Company served the wharves for many years until they closed in March 1972. In the redevelopment the entrance from Shad Thames with its fine columns have been retained.

Butlers Wharf and Anchor Brewhouse

The Design Museum

Conversion and Conservation

The warehouses, were converted to apartments and a dozen penthouses behind the original listed facade. There are five separate entrance halls each named after a 19th century clipper - Grassmere, Pebina, Paramatta, Hawkesbury and Tamar. The huge double-storey penthouses are with vast terraces and a conservatory. There are massive floor to ceiling timber columns, exposed brickwork and the traditional warehouse small pane, arched windows. Most of the bedrooms have large glazed warehouse doors, some of which open on to a cast-iron old gangway bridge, originally used to connect one warehouse to another. Other bridges have been added to extend the attractive vista along the whole of the pedestrianised street which replaced the old dockland canyon of Shad Thames.

The Design Museum

The Design Museum, opened in July 1989, is situated in the historic warehouses of Butlers Wharf. The Museum, created by the Conran Foundation, exhibits the growth of the design process and explains how design and technology influenced mass production, commerce and culture over the years. It has a number of broad thematic sections including chairs, office, home and transport. The Museum is another facet of London's leisure, educational and recreational facility for tourists and Londoners alike. There is a gallery for temporary exhibitions on the evolution of design and graphics. The Museum offers special educational programmes for schools and colleges with facilities of a lecture hall, workshops and a reference library for the public.

Shad Thames and canyon bridges

Butlers Wharf

THE CIRCLE AND HORSELYDOWN SQUARE

The Circle

The Circle is a large new residential development of over 300 apartments and penthouses complexes with shop and office units near Tower Bridge. A bronze dray horse sculpture stands at the central entrance of the scheme in Queen Elizabeth Street. The dominating feature of the design is a spectacular circular courtyard with towers, faced in nautical blue brick, rising to eight stories and adding a striking look to the entrance and the skyline. Situated in the Butlers Wharf Conservation Area, the character of the surrounding Victorian warehouses is reflected in the design of the new facade. All apartments have balconies which are arranged in steps producing a diagonal effect across the building. [6]

Courage Brewery Stables

The Courage Brewery Stables occupied the site of the Circle since early 1800 until 1985, although the area has been associated with horse grazing since the sixteenth century, hence the nearby Horselydown Lane. This name derives from "Horse-lie-down" or "Horseye-downe" on the map of the area dated 1544. The historical association with horses is commemorated by the larger than life bronze statue of a brewery Dray Horse which stands on a stone plinth in the middle of Queen Elizabeth Street at the centre of the development.

Horselydown Square

The Horselydown Square is a combination of new buildings and refurbishment, to the south of Butlers Wharf which provide a wide range of facilities including apartments, houses, restaurants/pubs, shops, offices and workshops, a fitness centre, new walkways and landscaped courtyards. Horselydown Square is located east of Tower Bridge and bounded by Shad Thames, Lafone Street, Gainsford Street and Horselydown Lane. The scheme adjoins Butlers Wharf. [4]

Eagle Wharf

The nearby listed Victorian tea warehouse has been converted into apartments with large balconies overlooking the Horselydown Square plaza.

Horselydown Square facing Butlers Wharf

ST SAVIOUR'S DOCK CONSERVATION AREA

St Saviour's Dock

Just down from Tower Bridge, past Butlers Wharf is the fascinating St. Saviour's Dock and the area around Mill Street where there is a delightful mixed area of some excellent warehouses conversions. St Saviour's Dock is a narrow and historic dock which once formed the mouth of the River Neckinger. In medieval times the area was honeycombed with canals which fed into the River Neckinger and gradually built into a dock. The beautiful high warehouses rising on either side have been restored to provide magnificent homes, offices, etc. Existing loading bays and the heavy timber door frames have been retained to form balconies for the flats. The conservation area includes Christian's Wharf, Vogan Mill and New Concordia Wharf.

Christians Wharf

Charming, Grade 2 listed, Victorian tea and spice warehouses at the western side of St. Saviour's Dock were converted in 1988 into luxury apartments and penthouses. The properties retain the old charm of the original building. The majority of the apartments have waterfront views. The painted lucams, projecting boxes formerly fitted with hoists and used to load goods into the warehouse loopholes below, have been retained and used as extensions to the upper apartments. [7]

Lloyds Wharf

Lloyds Wharf towers over the south eastern end of St. Saviour's Dock and was at one time a factory for manufacturing biscuit tins. The units were originally sold as 'shells' for buyers to convert as they wish. Consequently no two flats look the same.

Unity Wharf

Unity Wharf is a warehouse conversion north of Lloyds Wharf with large loft apartments and balconies overlooking St. Saviour's Dock.

Dockhead

This is a courtyard complex of offices, shops and apartments on a small site in the south east corner of St. Saviours Dock. It includes the conversion of the Victorian Italian Building and the construction of new surrounding buildings, creating an interesting commercial environment. [9]

Christians Wharf and St. Saviours Dock looking north

VOGAN MILL CONSERVATION AREA

New Mill Wharf (Vogan Mill)

The Vogan Mill in Mill Street of Bermondsey visually dominates the area with its new white tower soaring above the converted old warehouses and has superb views of the city. There is an impressive pillared entrance lobby. The six linked buildings, including four Grade 2 listed warehouses, offer 65 apartments, some with the original massive ceiling oak beams.

Vogan Mill can trace its origins back to the 16th century. In 1554, monks from the nearby Bermondsey Abbey built a small grain mill at a point where the old tributary, the River Neckinger, fed into the Thames. The Abbey did not survive Henry VIII's abolition of the monasteries. Gradually other buildings were built by merchants and the area came to be known as St. Saviour's Dock. During the 19th century Vogan added a wood hoop factory, a brewery and a slating factory. Vogan Mill became renowned in the Port of London as a centre for grain and the grinding of exotic spices from the East and West Indies.

Sufferance Wharf

This is a courtyard style of development along Tooley Street, of apartments and penthouses with some retail and office space overlooking the southern end of St. Saviour's Dock. The name of the development dates back to Elizabethan times when the Sufferance Wharves were licensed for the landing of goods which were the overspill from the congested "Legal Quays" on the north bank of the river between London Bridge and the Tower of London.

New Mill Wharf

New Concordia Wharf interior

Christians Wharf overlooking St. Saviour's Dock

NEW CONCORDIA WHARF CONSERVATION AREA

New Concordia Wharf

New Concordia Wharf is a group of Victorian Warehouses, a mill and water tower on the south bank of the River Thames on the eastern corner of the entrance to the old St Saviour's Dock in Bermondsey, about half a kilometre downstream of Tower Bridge. Built in 1885, these magnificent examples of riverside warehouses, Grade 2 listed, were one of the most renowned early conversions in Docklands. They are judged by the Historic Buildings Council to be an outstanding feature in the St Saviour's Dock Conservation Area.

The original interior structure of the building has been retained. Iron columns support timber beams and joists with timber floor boards. To satisfy the fire regulations in the conversion of the building, concrete slabs were inserted on top of the floor boards. The beautiful timber ceilings have been retained. On the exterior the existing loading bay doors and frames are unaltered. New metal windows similar to the original iron frames have been fitted. The large electric wall cranes of 1934 were retained to keep the historic appearance of the building. The water tower provides a magnificent apartment with commanding views of the River and London. A roof garden has been created within the area for the water tank on top.

Past History

St Saviour's Dock was originally the outlet of the River Neckinger, which was diverted along Jacob Street in the seventeenth century to create 'Jacob's Island, described as a notorious place by Charles Dickens in his novel 'Oliver Twist',

published in 1838. New Concordia Wharf was built later by Mr Seth Taylor in 1885. He was a wealthy grain merchant and named the buildings New Concordia Wharf after a town called Concordia, near Kansas City, Missouri, USA, from where much of the grain was imported and stored in the warehouses.

In 1934 Taylor sold the buildings to the nearby Butlers Wharf Company who undertook not to use the buildings for flour or provender milling so long as this did not restrict "chipping oats and barley, screening barley for malting, or polishing beans, peas or seeds"! In 1937 the large cranes were added to the Dock side and the buildings became Tea Warehouses. Between 1950 and 1980 they were turned to mixed warehouse use and, in addition to tea, stored rubber, paper, film, etc. The buildings have also been used in a number of films and television productions, including 'The French Lieutenant's Woman'.

New Concordia Wharf along Mill Street

New Concordia Wharf

Restoration and Conversion

The complete restoration and conversion of these superb buildings have created luxury flats varying in sizes, mostly with balconies over the River or Dock on the first to fifth floor. On the fifth and sixth floors, there are large penthouses with private roof garden terraces and excellent views of the Thames and City skyline. There are office suites, studio workshops on the first to third floors and a large restaurant on the ground floor, by the waters edge with direct access to the jetties. All units were completed to "shell finish" and fitted out by individual purchasers. A car park is provided at basement level. The development has other amenities including an indoor swimming pool.

The "Happy"

The Chairman of Jacob's Islands Company responsible for the renovation of New Concordia Wharf has his office on The Happy a former Edwardian HM Customs & Excise pontoon vessel which is reached by a walkway from the adjoining China Wharf.

China Wharf

China Wharf is a new residential building on the east side of New Concordia Wharf and is recognized from the river by its partly red facade.

Jacob's Island

It is a mixed residential and commercial development on the site of the original Jacob's Island known as Folly Ditch, described by Charles Dickens in Oliver Twist as being surrounded by a muddy ditch, six or eight feet deep and 15 to 20 feet wide when the tide is in. Those who wanted to live there must have power motives for a secret resident recorded Dickens. The scheme incorporates marine motifs such as overhanging balconies and sharp bow-shaped angles. [10]

China Wharf adjacent to New Concordia Wharf

Jacob's Island and Mill Street

CHERRY GARDEN PIER

Cherry Garden Pier

A short distance down river from St. Saviour's Dock is Cherry Garden Pier. This was named after an 18th century pleasure garden before it became an important shipping spot. Part of this stretch of river has been developed for both rented and private housing. Cherry Garden Pier in Bermondsey comprises a development of fine red brick terraces of houses named after Admirals Collingwood, Cornwallis, Calder and Barham and apartment blocks called Nelson, Hamilton and Hardy. The streets are tree lined with cobbled walkways. During the 17th and 18th centuries, the river pier used to be the landing place for spa resorts and nearby Chalybeate Springs frequented by Pepys. It is a stop for the Thamesline Riverbus.   [11]

The Angel Public House

The Angel, near Cherry Garden Pier, dates back to the 15th century when hospitality was served by the monks of Bermondsey Priory. In the 18th century it became the haunt of smugglers and famous personalities like Captain Cook. The 400 year old riverside tavern comprises oak beams, low ceilings and pillars and a superb view of the river and the lower Pool of London. The upstairs restaurant has dark wood panelling, lanterns and a ship's figurehead. Rotherhithe Tube Station is within a short walking distance.

Archaeological Site

This site, adjacent to The Angel, contains the remains of King Edward III's moated manor house.

Wilson Grove Conservation Area

The Wilson Grove Garden Village Estate, near Cherry Garden Pier, was built between 1924 and 1928 by the Bermondsey Borough Council. The small estate was one of the first council estates to provide assisted housing. Approached either from Bermondsey Wall East or Jamaica Road, the attractive cottage-style estate forms a pleasant group of dwellings.

The Angel Public House and Cherry Garden Pier

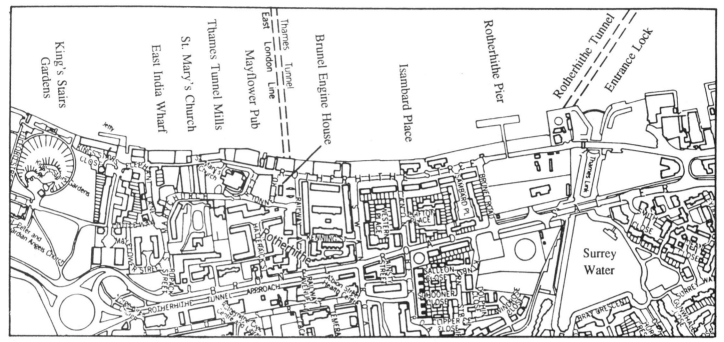

Map of St. Mary's Conservation Area and Surrey Water

Thames Tunnel Mills

THAMES TUNNEL MILLS AND ST MARY'S CONSERVATION AREA

St. Mary's Conservation Area

This conservation area, designated as of 'outstanding' beauty, is centred around St. Mary's church in Rotherhithe close to the underground station. Built by local shipbuilders in 1715 on the remains of an older one of Saxon times, it features tree-trunk pillars and a barrel shaped roof structure similar to the hull of an upturned ship! It has an octagonal obelisk spire. The original interior has shallow vaulted ceiling and tall columns.

Thames Tunnel Mills

Thames Tunnels Mills is a fine example of early 19th century Thameside warehouse architecture which is situated in the St. Mary's Church Conservation Area. Within the listed brick facades a new structure was constructed to provide 71 flats to be let at fair rents by the London and Quadrant Housing Trust. Built as a flour mill, its seven storeys rise up sheer from the river wall. A grant from the Historic Buildings Council financed the preservation of the outstanding features of the building. The original cast iron columns and timber beams have been used to form an atrium roofed over by a glass conservatory at sixth floor level with surrounding roof garden. The 80ft (24m) high free standing chimney and the original silo tower have been retained. The latter contains the passenger lift and is topped by the original cast iron water tank. **[16]**

The Mayflower Public House

A 17th century riverside alehouse, previously called the Skippe Inn, is adjacent to Thames Tunnel Mills in Rotherhithe which was a centre for shipbuilding in the old days. In 1620 the sailing ship The Mayflower moored here prior to her departure to Plymouth and then to America with the Pilgrim Fathers. The interior has original beams from the ship and wooden carvings. The inn is the only one in England licensed to sell both British and American postage stamps. The pub was partly rebuilt to house the Pilgrim's Restaurant and New Settler's bar.

Mayflower Court, Elephant Lane

Located within St. Mary's Conservation Area and east of King's Stairs Garden, these four storey red brick buildings have a typical London terraced theme for design. The larger houses are fronting and overhanging the river with views of Tower Bridge and the City to the west. A public walkway along the river frontage links up Prince's Stairs with the historical King's Stairs Gardens.

The Mayflower Public House, Rotherhithe Street

St. Mary's Conservation Area

ISAMBARD PLACE AND BRUNEL PUMPHOUSE MUSEUM

Isambard Place

Isambard Place is a residential development of properties situated on the bank of the Thames near Rotherhithe Tube Station and close to Surrey Water lake. Once known as Redriff, Rotherhithe has a long tradition in maritime activities. In the 17th century the Pilgrim Fathers set sail from near here for Plymouth to begin their voyage to America. Most of the crew of the ship, the Mayflower, were Rotherhithe residents. The external elevation of the development consists of yellow bricks with wrought iron balconies and slated roofs.   [19]

Atlas Reach

This housing estate is across the road from Isambard Place. Their "Kingston" maisonette won an award for the interior design with its space enhancing galleried bedroom.   [23]

Brunel Pumphouse Museum

The first tunnel under the River Thames was built by Sir Marc Isambard Brunel and his son Isambard Kingdom Brunel and was completed in 1843. It is now only used by underground trains, but it is still a perfect feat of civil engineering work by two distinguished engineers of the period. Part of the original tunnel together with the original stairs and handrails can be seen at Wapping Station on the north bank. The Engine House built in 1842, formerly housed the steam driven water pumps to drain water during the construction of the Thames Tunnel, is now a museum off Rotherhithe Street near Thames Tunnel Mills. The exhibition describes the process of construction of the tunnel and the associated events. The tunnel was the first of its kind in the world.

Renforth Pump House

The Pump House comprises a group of Grade 2 listed Victorian buildings of the former hydraulic pumping station in Renforth Street, only few minutes walk from Rotherhithe Station. The development, adjoining Surrey Quays, includes apartments, houses and offices with landscaped courtyards and a restored chimney. Twenty four apartments are provided in a 13 storey octagonal tower in a post-Italian renaissance style. The pumping station was built in 1902 by the London Power Company to supply the Surrey Commercial Docks.   [21]

Renforth Pump House   St Mary's Church, Rotherhithe

SURREY WATER AND KING & QUEEN WHARF

Surrey Water

Surrey Water, now part of a linking waterway with Canada Water, is a picturesque place, enhanced by the lake, canal, bridges and walkways. Part of the old Surrey Canal Docks, the adjacent entrance basin and lock at Rotherhithe were built in 1807.

Stave Hill

Half of this development of 109 properties in Rotherhithe were sold under the affordable scheme, so local residents were able to buy below market prices. Stave Hill is a made-up hill 18m high.   [24e]

Hithe Point

New waterside homes, called Hithe Point, were completed early 1990. The estate consists of over 200 flats and houses on the edge of Surrey Basin, the focal point of Rotherhithe redevelopment. The area has been transformed with canals and bridges giving it a delightful Amsterdam-style atmosphere. It is within walking distance of Surrey Quays shopping Superstore.   [24h]

King & Queen Wharf

A riverside block of flats in Rotherhithe Street with balconies and terraces from which to enjoy the river panorama. The building is constructed of London Stock brick with pediments and keystones in stone and a roof in natural slate. The river frontage encompasses internal courts and paved walkways. There is access to the Thames through arched steps and ramps. An elegant clocktower houses a lift providing access to the internal courts. Rotherhithe Station is close.   [71]

Globe Wharf

The riverside Globe Wharf adjacent to King and Queen Wharf, the largest rice warehouse was in use until 1983. The conversion of this wharf incorporates a central atrium and includes a retail and leisure complex. Surrounding the central atrium there are 140 apartments still retaining many of the original features of the old warehouse.

The City from Stave Hill

King & Queen Wharf and Globe Wharf

LAVENDER POND NATURE PARK

The Pump House and Lavender Pond

Lavender Pond used to be a shallow lake where timber from the Surrey Docks was floated for temporary storage. Small boats and lighters would enter the pond through Lavender Lock. This entrance was blocked in 1928 when the Pump House was built by the Port of London Authority to maintain water levels in the former Surrey Commercial Docks. The impressive building acts as a centre for a small nature reserve locally. The entrance is in Lavender Road off Rotherhithe Street. **[64]**

Lavender Wharf

Lavender Wharf is a five acre site in Rotherhithe Street. The scheme consists of homes along a superb quarter-mile river frontage, with views across the Thames. **[66]**

Acorn Walk

Built in the 1930s for housing the dockers by the London Borough of Southwark, the blocks of flats have pantiled gambrel roofs, bow-ended balconies and two-tone yellow and red brick walls. Two of the blocks contain fair rent flats. The Art Deco exteriors of the buildings have been restored. They are near Nelson Dock on the eastern side of Surrey Docks. **[61]**

Stave Hill Ecological Park

There is a wildlife trail from Lavender Pond Nature Park south to Russia Dock Woodland and Stave Hill Ecological Park at the centre of the Surrey Docks peninsular. The 2.2 hectare park contains grass land with different types of shrubs and surrounded by ash and maple woodland. There are also two ponds near the middle of the site. A variety of birds including goldfinches, wagtails and warblers are resident. Several families of foxes inhabit the area. From the adjacent Stave Hill there are beautiful views of the City, Wapping, Limehouse, the Isle of Dogs, the Royal Docks and the Surrey Docks.

Lavender Pond Nature Park, Rotherhithe

Hithe Point housing

COLUMBIA WHARF/ LAURENCE WHARF AND NELSON DOCK

Scandic Crown Hotel

London Docklands first new international hotel, the four-star Scandic Crown Hotel opened in March 1991. Situated on the south side of the River Thames, right opposite the new Canary Wharf development, the 390 bedroom hotel consists of three buildings including Nelson House, the converted listed Columbia warehouse and two new blocks. A small Victorian engine house has been converted into a museum incorporating the original machinery for Nelson Dock.   [60]

Nelson House

The historic Nelson House, Grade 2 listed and from 1740, is full of interesting architectural features and is in its original form. At the top of the house there is an exclusive apartment called the "Crows Nest". The building is used as a VIP conference centre and contains a small shop.

Columbia Wharf

In the dry dock in the middle of the hotel site is situated a replica of a 19th century French sailing/sea going barge and now serves as a gourmet seafood restaurant. Nearby is the "Battle of Copenhagen" a riverhouse bar, complete with red painted floor and just like the gundeck of Nelson's ship. International cuisine is served at the restaurant with the atmosphere of the original Columbria Wharf building featuring old brick walls and wooden ceiling beams. Columbia Wharf warehouse building was originally used for storage of grain imported from the British Commonwealth countries. The Nordic Conference Centre features a large multi-purpose exhibition and conference room and seats up to 400 with smaller meeting and syndicate rooms. The new pier at Nelson

Dock is linked to the reception building by glass sided walkways one of which leads to the Battle of the Nile club which is a health and leisure centre.

Old Nelson Dry Dock

Nelson dry dock was a small ship repair yard and had a slipway up which vessels were pulled by a reciprocating engine which has been preserved. The ship would be drawn a short distance at a time by the revolving crank shaft. Between 1750 and 1820 Nelson Dock was one of three yards which were used for steamship building. From 1850 the yard built clippers for the China tea trade.

Nelson House

Scandic Crown Hotel at Nelson Dock

Laurence Wharf

On the south side of the Thames, opposite Canary Wharf, the Danish designed development is clearly visible from the Isle of Dogs. Laurence Wharf was built around the listed 18th century Nelson Dry Dock, just off Rotherhithe Street in the Surrey Docks. The former barge berth, was destroyed by bombing during the second world war. The dry dock has been converted into a marina of 90 berths with a crane to lift boats in and out and get access to the Thames without heavy port charges. The development consists of two blocks, Leander Court and Alexander Court after the ships of the line commanded by Nelson in the battle of Copenhagen of 1801. The mirror image buildings are on each side of the marina. The other two buildings of the scheme comprise the listed Columbia Wharf warehouses and three adjoining former workshop buildings which have been converted into luxury apartments and a leisure complex as part of the Scandic Crown Hotel.

There was a conscious effort not to replicate the traditional warehouse architecture but to blend into the existing waterside warehouses that stretch along the river in Docklands. The basic facing material is yellow stock brick imported directly from Denmark framing large windows and private balconies. Lightweight penthouses top the riverside and southern buildings. [60]

Rotherhithe and the Surrey Docks

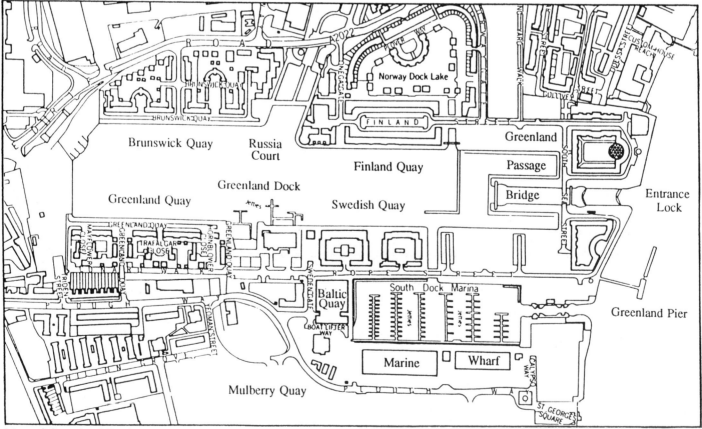

Map of Greenland Dock

GREENLAND DOCK AND BRUNSWICK QUAY

Greenland Dock looking west

Greenland Dock

Greenland Dock has been at the centre of an amazing transformation of the Surrey Docks with numerous housing schemes and riverside developments, together with the Surrey Quays retail centre to the west of the dock. Housing developments of Brunswick Quay, Russia Court, Finland Quay, Norway Yard and Norway Dock line up the north bank of the dock. The area between the dock water and the River Thames has eight-storey buildings known as Greenland Passage. To the south side are Greenland Quay, the Water Sports Centre, and Swedish Quays. The lock passages and river front have been landscaped as public areas. Surrey Quays Station of the East London Line is a short distance to the south west of the Dock.

Brunswick Quay

Brunswick Quay on the north western side of Greenland Dock, was one of the first housing development of flats and town houses with mooring facilities in the Surrey Docks. The public areas were paved and blended with tree planting along the quayside. [31]

Greenland Quay

This is a residential estate of affordable homes which directly overlook Greenland Dock. The buildings are set back from the water and their height has been designed to ensure adequate wind patterns around the dock to meet the needs for sailing and other water sports. During the 18th century Greenland Dock was used by the Greenland Whaling Company. By the 1800s whaling had died and the main trade for the dock until its closure in the late 1960s was timber from the Scandinavian countries. [35]

Russia Court and Finland Quay from Greenland Quay

GREENLAND PASSAGE AND FINLAND QUAYS

Greenland Passage

Greenland Passage boasts an enviable position at the mouth of Greenland Dock and all the properties enjoy delightful water views over the Dock and the River Thames. Greenland Passage lies at the eastern end of Greenland Dock, with the lock entrance dividing the development. Each of the two halves has been designed as an enclosure around a greenspace with buildings varying from two to five stories. They comprise flats and town houses up to five bedrooms in size. Portland stone and yellow stock bricks have been used for the external facing. The main entrance lock is Grade 1 listed, and has many of the original features, such as the hydraulic capstans and rams. The old pedestrian steel bridge has also been beautifully restored to provide a right of way. Greenland Passage Pier for the Riverbus is just south of the development. [42]

Finland Quays East and West

Finland Quay is a waterfront development of apartments and three bedroom duplexes with beautiful views of Greenland Dock. The site was part of the former trading quay for the import of softwood from Scandinavia and the Baltic. [43/45]

Russia Court East & West

This complex occupies a quayside site on the north side of Greenland Dock bounded to the south and east by water. The scheme has four areas to provide a mix of commercial and residential properties including a dockside public house. The seven storey residential blocks are flanked by raised terraces on the quayside. [33/34]

Lower Odessa Wharf

This is a conversion of an old warehouse of masonry walls and timber floors to provide commercial and leisure facilities.[50]

New Caledonia Wharf

New Caledonia Wharf is alongside the Thames and north of Greenland Passage and contains a complex of apartments with a swimming pool, bar, gymnasium and sauna plus lavish decor. The entrance foyer is described as having a New York style with an added hint of art deco, with banded Nash-style plasterwork sponged with grey and creamy white set off with dark grey and brown. [51]

Greenland Passage and Pier

The old pedestrian bridge across Greenland entrance lock

NORWAY DOCK AND SURREY DOCKS FARM

The Lakes, Norway Dock

Townhouses, villas and apartments at the Lakes, are on the eastern side of the Surrey peninsular. Norway Dock has a re-excavated lake and adjoins Greenland Dock. It was originally built adjoining Greenland Dock for the whaling trade in the late eighteenth century and was subsequently used by ships importing timber from Scandinavia. In 1969 the dock was closed and in the following year it was filled in. Traditional brick is used throughout and roofs of natural slate. Many of the villas are at the lake's edge, with some entirely surrounded by water and approached only by timber pontoons.   [44]

Lady Dock

Lady Dock, situated in Redriff Road and part of the Downtown Community in Rotherhithe, is named after the dock built in 1811. At the western boundary of the housing estate, there is a tree-lined strip which gives access to the public open space created from the filled-in Russia Dock.   [46]

Surrey Docks City Farm

The City Farm is located on the eastern side of Surrey Docks and overlooks the River Thames. The one and a half hectare farm has housing for a variety of animals including pigs, goats, chickens, ducks, donkeys and sheep. It has a class room and all visitors are welcome. This provides a valuable education and community resource to local schools and others. Visitors can purchase cheese, eggs and honey.   [53]

Russia Dock Woodland

To the west of the Surrey Docks Farm, lies the Russia Dock Woodland and Park which includes a dense planting of trees of various species such as willows and poplars. The park laid on the former infilled Russia Dock forms a nature trail from Lavender Pond to Greenland Dock with streams and marshland. In the marshy vegetation along the edge of the woodland you can see frogs spawning in the spring. Moorhens are also often seen in the marsh and the mallard duck in the water.

Surrey Docks City Farm

SOUTH DOCK MARINA AND SWEDISH QUAY

Marine Wharf

A mixed commercial, residential and leisure complex was established within the only surviving Warehouses 1 and 3 of the former Surrey Docks. Built in 1938, they are of reinforced concrete frame with brick infill and were used in the old days for general warehousing. **[38]**

Mulberry Quay

This is a conversion of the former Port of London Authority Police Station at South Dock into a public house, restaurant and marina club. The building is of traditional brick construction dating back to early this century. During the Second World War, Greenland and South Docks became a centre for building the famous large concrete structures "Mulberry Harbours" which were floated across the channel to France to provide temporary harbours for the Allied forces landing. **[39]**

Swedish Quay

Swedish Quay is set in two quadrangles on a peninsular with water on three sides. The east elevation is along Steel Yard Cut, the canal which connects Greenland Dock to South Dock. Externally, the elevations and roofscape artistically reflect the sail shapes of ships which once used the docks. **[40]**

Baltic Quay

Baltic Quay, which stands on the west side of the South Dock Marina, punctuates the overall Surrey Docks area with its barrel vaulted six storey podium adjoining a 14 storey tower. The development offers a mix of residential, retail and office accommodation. The business space comprises two floors overlooking a courtyard with views of the marina. The waterside building is a glass clad steel frame for optimum levels of natural light. **[41]**

Marine Wharf

South Dock Marina and Baltic Quay

SURREY QUAYS SHOPPING PRECINCT AND ASSOCIATED NEWS WORKS

Surrey Quays Shopping Precinct

Docklands' first super shopping centre, close to Surrey Quays Tube Station, was opened to the public in October 1988. The precinct has been developed by Tesco on a 9 hectare site adjacent to Canada Water at the south western part of the peninsula of the Surrey Docks about 2 km east of Tower Bridge. The scheme provides a Tesco Superstore, a British Home Store, a food court and 34 other shops. There is a strong emphasis on fashion. Surrey Quays has a nautical appearance in keeping with its waterside location. Life-belts, ropes and rigging have been displayed to emphasize the atmosphere. At the centre of the scheme is a full height atrium complete with pool foundations and a 3 metre high bronze dolphin sculpture. Two ground floor glass roofed malls stretch in opposite directions from the atrium to the two anchor units at either end of the centre. At first floor level overlooking the central square is the galleried Quays Food Court.   [30]

Historic Dock Offices

The Dock Manager's office was built by the Surrey Commercial Dock Company in 1887, and it continued in use up to the closure of the docks in 1969. The beautiful Victorian buildings were restored by the Docklands Development Corporation for use as their area office. It is one of the last few remaining links with the original docks. It is located adjacent to Surrey Quays Shopping Precinct and overlooks Canada Water Lake.

Associated News Works

The Mail Newspaper printing works were established in 1984 in the middle of the Surrey Docks and are one of the most modern in Europe, from which all its publications are produced. The centre comprises a reel store; press hall, publishing hall and administrative building.   [29]

Surrey Quays Centre

There are proposals for a major development of offices, commerical, retail, residential and leisure facilities around Canada Water Lake. Together with the existing Tesco Shopping precinct, they will create a new commercial focus for the area.   [28]

Surrey Docks Offices

Surrey Quays Shopping Centre

THE ROYAL DOCKS

The Great Docks

The Royal Docks, consisting of the Royal Victoria, Royal Albert and King George V Docks, have an area the size of Central London from Hyde Park in the west to Tower Bridge in the east. They are unique in the large scale of their water environment. They contain the largest remaining development area in Docklands. In Beckton, the northern part, there has been substantial house building since 1981. To the south are 270 hectares (550 acres) of docklands with 120 hectares of water and 16 km of quayside awaiting development. With its waterscape and transport links the area is ripe for mixed-use regeneration.

For over a century, the Royal Docks were the centre of world trade and at the hub of the British Empire. Ships would be lined more than three deep and the quaysides echoed to the sounds of dockers as they loaded and discharged cargoes from the farthest corners of the earth. They were truly the great storehouses of the world. Like the rest of the docks they declined in the late 1960s and subsequently closed.

Plan for Regeneration

The present plan for regeneration is centred on the implementation of three large schemes proposed by a private developers' consortia. Existing outline planning permission include regional shopping facilities, business parks including hi-tech manufacturing and research, huge arena and exhibition space, hotel and leisure development, office complexes, housing and sport facilities.

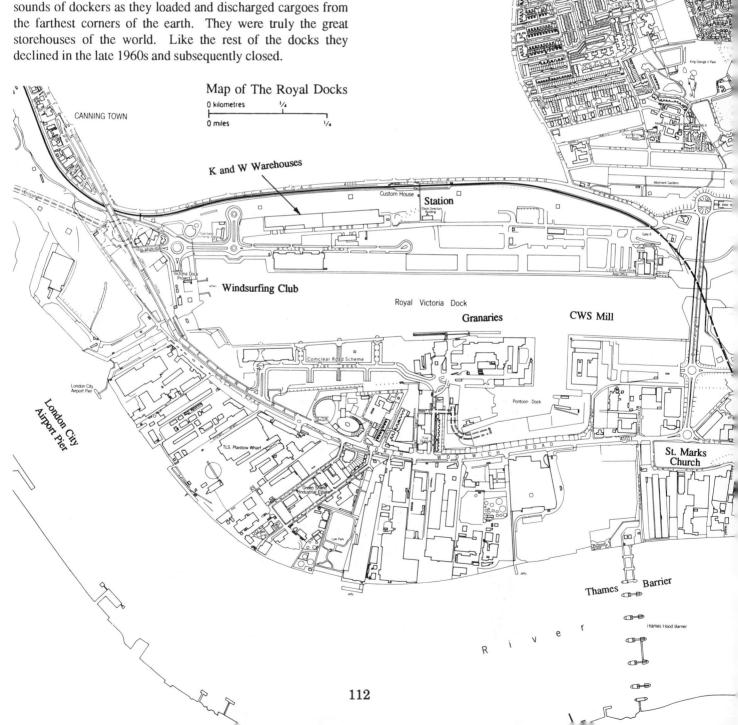

Map of The Royal Docks

112

The Londondome on the north side of the Royal Victoria Dock, is to provide a multi-use arena and exhibition space together with a mixed development of housing, retail, leisure and hotels. On the south side there are proposals for hotel and leisure, a business park and residential developments.

BECKTON

Beckton

CYPRUS

Dock Manager's Office

Royal   Albert   Dock

Gallions Hotel

Albert Basin

Runway

London   City   Airport

King   George   V   Dock

Waterski Club

NORTH WOOLWICH

Tate & Lyle
Pier

T h a m e s

Woolwich
Ferry

N. Woolwich
Railway Museum

Royal Victoria
Gardens

LONDON DOCKLANDS
THE ROYAL DOCKS

Tidal Basin Pumping Station

Tate & Lyle

Location Map of The Royal Docks

Royal Albert Dock, Spine Road and Docklands Light Railway Extension, well underway.

Connaught Crossing under construction, linking the north and south areas of the Royal Docks.

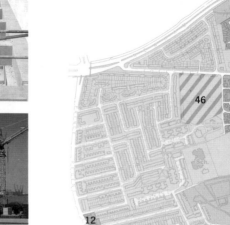

Major infrastructure and redevelopment work is taking place on a mammoth scale throughout the Royal Docks area.

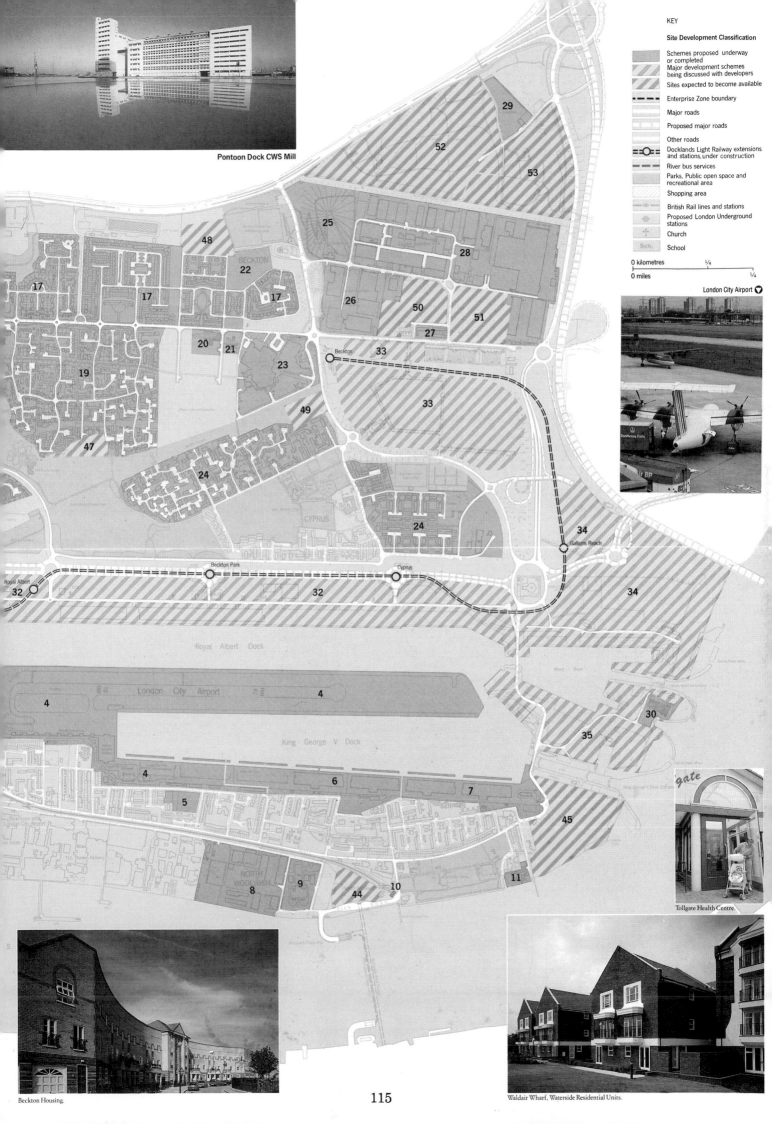

Pontoon Dock CWS Mill

BECKTON

CYPRUS

Beckton

Beckton Park

Cyprus

Royal Albert

Gallions Reach

Royal   Albert   Dock

London City Airport

King George V Dock

NORTH WOOLWICH

Tollgate Health Centre.

Beckton Housing.

Waldair Wharf, Waterside Residential Units.

LONDON DOCKLANDS
THE ROYAL DOCKS

LOCATION MAP FEATURE NUMBERS

The features described in this section of the book are numbered as listed below and the locations are shown by the corresponding numbers on the map on the previous page.

1.	Green Shield Industrial Estate	27.	Crescent Terrace
2.	St Marks Industrial Estate	28.	London Industrial Park
3.	Museum of Victorian Life	29.	Strategic Lorry Park
4.	London City Airport	30.	Newham Community College
5.	St Edwards	31.	Royal Victoria Dock North
6.	King George V Dock - South Side	32.	Royal Albert Dock North
7.	King George V Dock - South Side	33.	Windsor Park Housing and Proposed School
8.	Standard Industrial Estate	34.	Eastern Gateway
9.	British Telecom Teleport	35.	Albert Basin
10.	North Woolwich Railway Museum	36.	The Limmo Site
11.	Waldair Wharf and Bargehouse Road	37.	Thames Wharf
12.	New Housing	38.	Royal Victoria Dock South (Comclear)
13.	LB Newham Housing or School Site	39.	Pontoon Dock
14.	The Chestnuts	40.	CWS Mill
15.	West Beckton	41.	Thames Barrier lands
16.	Park Quays	42.	The Connaught Site
17.	North Beckton Sites 1, 2 & 3	43.	Oriental Road Site
18.	Ellen Wilkinson School	44.	North Woolwich Station Site
19.	Mid Beckton	45.	Gallions Point Site
20.	St Marks Church & Community Centre	46.	West Beckton Site 3
21.	Tollgate Health Centre	47.	Mid Beckton
22.	North Beckton Site 3	48.	North Beckton Site 3D
23.	Beckton District Centre	49.	Beckton Corridor Site
24.	Cyprus	50.	Alpine Way Site
25.	Beckton Alps & Ski Slope - Mountaintop	51.	The County Road Site
26.	Beckton Retail Park	52.	Triangle Site
		53.	Triangle Site Extension

The Royal Docks looking west

BECKTON

Beckton Housing

One of the first areas to be developed in Docklands in the early 1980s, Beckton lies to the North of the Royal Docks and south of the A13 and approximately 10 km from the City. Over three thousand family homes have been built in closes and winding streets, with many of the houses sold to local residents under the policy of providing affordable homes. The Docklands Light Railway eastern extension connects Beckton to Canary Wharf and the City of London.

Towards the end of the nineteenth century the Port of London expanded eastward with the construction of the Royal Group of Docks and the opening of the Eastern Counties Railway Line through Stratford. This led to the development of chemical industries, shipbuilding and gas manufacture in the area. The Gaslight and Coke Company built their works and named it Beckton after Simon Adam Beck then Governor of the company. The company built the world's largest coal/gas works which continued production until its closure in 1976 with the advent of North Sea gas.

Tollgate Square

Tollgate Square is a Georgian style development modelled on traditional London squares. The properties ranging from flats to four-bedroom town houses are set on gently curving terraces forming the square.

Beckton Alps

Beckton has an Asda Superstore including a covered shopping complex. Across the road stands Beckton Retail Park. Beckton Alps at the entrance to the Retail Park is a local landmark with its dry ski slope and views over the Royal Docks. Near Beckton Alps and off Newham Way is the world famous West Ham United Football Club. [25]

Beckton Alps Ski centre

Tollgate Mews

This is a Georgian crescent of three to five bedroom townhouses elegantly resembling that of Bath, Individual properties have gardens surrounded by wrought iron fencing.

Rail and spine road roller coaster through the Royal Docks looking west towards the City

ROYAL VICTORIA DOCK NORTH

The Age of Glory

Prince Albert opened the Royal Victoria Dock in 1855, the first of the large complex of docks which dominated the eastern part of London Docklands. Ships unloaded cargoes from across the world at the old "Vic fingers" quays, jutting into the water, a pattern which was filled-in during this century and is now being planned for restoration for housing and leisure. Plans for regeneration of the Victoria Dock include two large schemes proposed by private consortia on the north and south sides of the dock.

Master Plan For North Side

This scheme on the north side of the dock proposes a mixture of homes, offices, shops, leisure facilities and hotels. The largest component will be the Londondome, an indoor multi-purpose arena and exhibition hall. Housing piers will project into the dock like the old finger quays when the dock was first built. New pedestrian bridges will provide access from South Canning Town and Custom House into the new developments on the south side of the dock to West Silvertown. The Town Square and Town Dock will be the centre of the new community, with shops and public amenities. The area will be served by existing rail links at Custom House and the new Docklands Light Railway. The development will be phased and will take about ten years to complete. The office development includes high technology units and "flexible business space" zoned in and around the old K to S warehouses. About 1750 new homes are proposed with buildings into the dock. The proposed development is compatible with the use of the dock itself for sailing and other water sports. It will provide a waterside promenade with cafes and restaurants. The quayside will be opened to the public with walkways and parks. [31]

Londondome

The major part of the Royal Victoria Dock regeneration will be a large international exhibition and conference complex called Londondome which will occupy about half the land area of the site. The arena will be the focus of the project, seating 25,000 in permanent and temporary seating and using the most advanced technical equipment for presentation and transmission of shows, concerts and sporting events. The area will have direct access to the adjoining exhibition halls. The Londondome is considered to be the largest modern complex of its type proposed in London. There would be a 500 bed hotel and specialist shopping in a new Festival Market at three levels.

Proposed development of the Royal Victoria Dock

Sailing Basin

The western end of the dock will form a small sailing craft basin. It will be centred on a floating boathouse with a second floor cafe. The angled wharves will create a double-bow shape basin, which will have an 80 metre turning point at each end. A network of boat-lined canals around the housing piers will bring a Venice like setting.

Museum Dock

In front of the historic W Warehouse, restored barges, ships or a tugboat will be moored alongside a replica of the original waterfront as floating monuments to the old days of the dock. Masts would frame the cross dock and equipment from the working docks will be exhibited.

Town Dock

The focal point for the local communities would be this water square at the midpoint of the development framed by the Town Dock pier and east pedestrian bridge. The marina will have sailing boats.

Custom House Station

North of the Royal Victoria Dock, the Custom House Station is situated on the original Railway Line to North Woolwich which was opened in 1855 and is still in service. It will be integrated with the new development on the north side of the dock.

Connaught Tavern

The nearby Connaught Tavern in Connaught Road was designed by Vigers and Wagstaffe in 1881 and is a Grade 2 listed large public house in Queen Anne style. Outside the pub there is a Victorian cast iron urinal used by generations of dockers who worked in the Royal Docks. The pub was a popular meeting place for these dockers.

Tidal Basin Pumping Station

This new circular pumping station for drainage purposes has interesting architectural features and is located on the north west corner of the Victoria Dock.

The Connaught Tavern Public House

The proposed Londondome

ROYAL VICTORIA DOCK SOUTH

Master Plan for South Side

This area comprises some 50 hectares extending from St Mark's Church in the east to the infilled western lock of the dock and southward to the River Thames adjacent to the Thames Barrier. The main existing buildings are the large granaries around Pontoon Dock. Four main areas of redevelopment are proposed. The part to the west of the existing mill buildings, known as Comclear, will be predominately new housing. The area around Pontoon Dock will be of a mixed use character, including retail, offices, hotels, pubs, restaurants, cafes and watersport activities. These developments will be linked to the north side of the dock by a new pedestrian bridge. A water taxi service will also be established. To the east of Pontoon Dock will be a mix of offices, hi-tech and light industry. The Thames Barrier lands to the south will provide a new public garden of 10 hectares along the Thames. It will be approximately half the size of Green Park in Central London. **[38]**

Comclear Housing

Based upon a mixture of about 80 per cent flats and 20 per cent houses, up to 3000 new dwellings are proposed, primarily located at Comclear in the west and on the Barrier lands in the south. It is intended that there should be different types of housing tenure on the sites, subject to agreement with the London Borough of Newham and the relevant housing associations. A watersports centre will be established near the western entrance of the Victoria Dock.

Pontoon Dock Shopping

The major nucleus of shopping will be located on the west side of Pontoon Dock. The dockside development would include small supermarkets, restaurants, hotels, sports and chandlers stores. Studios to sell jewellery, pottery and art work are also proposed. Additional attractions proposed include boating facilities, restaurant and a visitor centre to the Thames Barrier. The riverside park and dock areas will be used for a variety of events and activities.

Business Park

Provision for office type development is located around and to the east of Pontoon Dock. It will include light industry and workspace units located in the east near London City Airport. The homebased work studios, with good retail outlets, will be part of or near to the refurbished mill buildings. Up to three hotels are planned to cater for the needs of the business park.

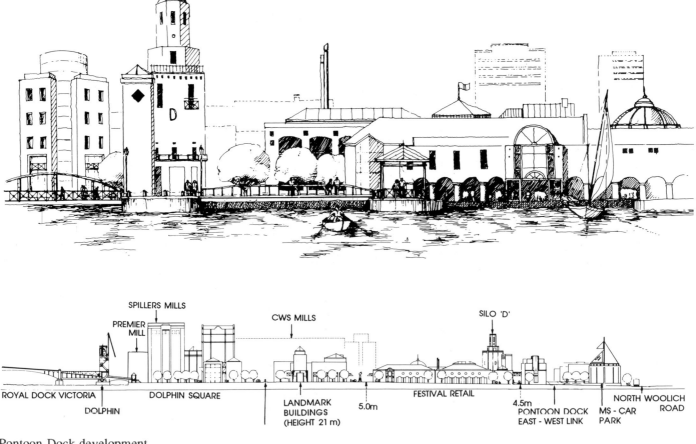

Pontoon Dock development.

GRAIN MILLS AND THAMES BARRIER

Pontoon Dock

The Pontoon Dock was built in 1855 on the south side of the Victoria Dock and was fitted with hydraulic lifts to raise ships out of water by a system of hydraulic jacks placed on pontoons which would be floated into the small finger docks for repair purposes. The fingers have been since filled in but they can be excavated to provide an attractive setting for new developments and a water sport centre. Another important feature of the dock is the historic octagonal building Silo D located on the south west corner of the dock, offering a unique development opportunity. [39]

Rank and Spillers Granaries

West of Pontoon Dock are three reinforced concrete buildings erected in the 1930s. The outer two in the complex were owned by Ranks and the middle one, Spillers Millenium Mills, is still operated by the London Borough of Greenwich. Adjacent to these granaries and directly overlooking the waters of the Victoria Dock, and the only link to the past, is the Premier Mill which is Grade 2 listed and dates back to 1860. The buildings are awaiting redevelopment as part of the south side of the Victoria Dock and may even be demolished.

CWS Mill

Situated on the south east side of the Victoria Dock, this massive white granary was built in reinforced concrete in the late 1930s to receive imported grain directly from ships. It was owned previously by the Co-operative Wholesale Society (CWS). Plans have been suggested to convert the building into a hotel but they could also be demolished. The granary replaced a late 19th century steam powered mill. [40]

Thames Flood Barrier

To the south of the Royal Victoria Dock lies the Thames Flood Barrier opened in 1984. It is one of the engineering wonders of the world, spanning 520m across the river with four main steel gates, each weighing 3700 tonnes and 61m wide. When closed the gates stand nearly 16m above the river bed. The Barrier can be closed within 30 minutes of a high surge forecast to protect London from flooding. The visitor centre on the south bank of the river at the Barrier Gardens Pier houses an excellent collection of working models and exhibitions with audio-visual shows.

The Thames Flood Barrier.

The old granaries south of the Royal Victoria Dock.

ROYAL ALBERT DOCK

Master Plans

Plans to redevelop the north and east side of the Royal Albert Dock intend to build over 250 homes, a massive business park, a marine centre and provision for a shopping centre in the Albert Dock Basin, subject to the decision to proceed with the proposed East London River Crossing. The redevelopment will include the historic buildings of Central Buffet, Dock Manager's Office and Gallions Hotel.   [32]

Central Buffet

A listed Grade 2 building, a former public house on the north side of Albert Dock, was designed by the architects Vigers and Wagstaffe in 1883 to afford facilities for ship passengers at the Royal Docks.

Dock Manager's Office

A similar listed building and adjacent to the Central Buffet, the attractive Dock Manager's Office is awaiting redevelopment. Both buildings can be seen from the new Royal Albert Dock spine road.

Gallions Hotel

This Grade 2 listed hotel in Gallions Road was built by the London and St. Katharine Dock Company during 1881-3 for use by passengers on the P & O Line. Designed by Vigers and Wagstaffe, the building was constructed on piles and had stables below the ground floor. It is awaiting restoration and possible relocation.

Albert Basin

The Albert Basin, the entrance basin for the Albert Dock opened in 1880, forms an attractive focal point for future developments. There are fine views of the River Thames and the two entrance locks of Gallions and King George V. Major retail development and leisure including a marina, waterside public house and restaurants are proposed. It is immediately adjacent to the proposed East London River Crossing. The Gallions Yacht Entrance Lock, 168m long by 24m wide, gives access to the basin from the river.   [35]

East London River Crossing

The bridge across the Thames is intended to open for operation in 1997 which will give London Docklands a road link to the Channel Tunnel and the European network.

The Central Buffet

The Dock Manager's office

KING GEORGE V DOCK

London City Airport

London City Airport (LCA), constructed on the quay between the Royal Albert Dock and King George V Dock, is an asset to any company moving to the Royals as well as a major booster for Docklands. It is designed to handle aircraft developed specifically for operating in urban areas and restricted sites. With the completion of the Leamouth Crossing and the Royal Docks spine road, the airport has direct links with Canary Wharf and the M11 motorway. The DLR eastern extension provides excellent services to the city. Further details are given on page 132. [4]

King George V Dock South

An area of 9 hectare to the south of King George V Dock extending to North Woolwich is planned for mixed use development. Part of the scheme will be for commercial and airport related activities. Another part is allocated for a residential scheme. [6]

Gallions Point

This site, formerly occupied by Harland & Wolff shipbuilding company, has a fine position on the bend of the River Thames with King George V Ship Lock built in 1921 to the north. Existing outline planning permissions include proposals for residential and retail developments. [45]

Waldair Wharf

This new residential development lies south of the Royal Docks and adjacent to the Royal Victoria Gardens. [11]

Royal Docks Water Sports

The Royal Docks offer excellent leisure activities which are water based. The Waterski Club at King George V Dock (telephone no 081-511-2000) has facilities for the experienced and the beginners with gradual introduction to the long tow rope used by the professionals. The exciting sport of wet biking involves whizzing over the water at speeds of up to 50 mph and is run by the Wetbike School, King George V Dock (telephone no 081-511-2000). Windsurfing is well established with the use of fibreglass sails that send windsurfers shooting along the surface of the water. This popular leisure pursuit is available at the Windsurfing Club, Royal Victoria Dock (telephone no 081-474-2500). Water sport races are held regularly at the Royal Victoria Dock. During 1988 an outdoor concert, called 'Destination Docklands', proved also popular.

Powerboat Racing at the Royal Victoria Dock

London City Airport

HISTORIC WAREHOUSES

K-S Warehouses

The K-S range of warehouses along the north side of the Royal Victoria Dock has a quarter of a mile of fine Georgian style brick elevation. The K Warehouse, built in 1858-59, is a Grade 2 listed building with a later addition of an annexe. The S warehouses date back to the 1920s and are not listed. The K warehouse is 98.4m long and 21.9m wide and was used in the old days for the storage of imported tobacco.

W Warehouse

Opposite the K-S Warehouses is another famous listed building, the W Warehouse, built in 1883 for storage of tobacco and currently used for the exhibition of the Museum in Docklands. The London Docklands Development Corporation wishes to dedicate this and the K-S Warehouses for use by the arts and media industries, both commercial and public-sponsored, and is seeking creative proposals for implementation. Memories of the shipping activities which once made the Victoria Dock one of the busiest and most modern in the world could be preserved along side the historic W Warehouse, where replica barges could be moored, together with artefacts and machinery on the quay.

The historic K Warehouse

The historic W Warehouse

St. Marks Church Museum of Victorian Life

MUSEUMS AND GARDENS

Museum in Docklands

The Museum in Docklands has a temporary housing in the W Warehouse in the Royal Docks. The museum has an excellent collection of old dock tools and machinery. The oldest piece from the dock era is an 1820 hand winch from the Cutler Street Warehouse. A unique item at present is a Roman docker's hook. It is the same as a modern pad hook and it was found during excavations on the north bank at Billingsgate where the Romans built the first wharves on the Thames. There are cast iron bits and pieces; machine gears, date roundals, bollards, valves, fairleads, pieces of hydraulic cranes and a number of other items, including moulds. There is also a barrow with handles at each end. It was said to be the official ambulance "to trundle off an injured docker to the hospital or knacker's yard"! There are everyday things from years ago including dockers' tallies from 1870. These were metal discs denoting a specific job, and given up at the end of the day so that the day's wages could be totted up. The museum must be fully supported to preserve Docklands heritage.

North Woolwich Railway Museum

The museum is housed in the North Woolwich old Railway Station which was opened in 1847 as part of the extension of the Eastern Counties Railway to North Woolwich. It contains many objects and features the history of the Great Eastern Railway, including a restored ticket office. The former booking hall and waiting rooms have displays of photographs documents, various objects and tickets. Some tracks have been re-laid with a Robert Stephenson and Hawthorn Engine at the platforms. The waiting rooms and booking hall reflect the golden age of the railways during the 1920s and 1930s.

Royal Victoria Gardens

Adjacent to North Woolwich Station, the park was opened in 1851 as a Victorian pleasure garden, following the opening of the London and Blackwall Railway with its terminus at North Woolwich.

St Mark's Church Museum

This remarkable church in Silvertown was built 1861-62 in hollow ceramic blocks, brick and stone to the design of the architect S.S. Teulon. It was destroyed by fire in the early 1980s but was restored and converted into a Museum of Victorian Life. It has a beautiful stone interior. [3]

The Museum in Docklands

North Woolwich Railway Museum

Communications

COMMUNICATIONS IN LONDON DOCKLANDS
Travel Map

KEY

	Major roads
	Proposed major roads
	Docklands Light Railway lines and stations.
	Docklands Light Railway extensions and stations, under construction
	Docklands Light Railway extensions and stations proposed
	River Bus services
	British Rail stations
	British Rail lines
	London City Airport
	Satellite stations
	London Underground stations existing
	London Underground stations proposed
	Central line
	Metropolitan line
	Hammersmith & City line
	District line
	Circle line
	Northern line
	East London line
	Jubilee line proposed Route

Map Produced for the L.D.D.C. by:
Geonex Story Ltd (Chartered Land Surveyors)
© Copyright L.D.D.C. June 1991

By Tube and Docklands Light Railway

126

DOCKLANDS LIGHT RAILWAY

The Docklands Light Railway (DLR) is Britain's first fully automated light rapid transit system. It is the primary artery of the public transport system in Docklands. The whole system connects with the London Underground network at Bank Station in the City. Bank to Canary Wharf takes about 10 to 15 minutes. By the middle of the 1990's it is estimated that 200,000 passengers will be using DLR daily.

DLR which opened in August 1987, has exceeded expectations with over 30,000 passengers per day being carried and has a continuing upward trend. Not only has its success created interest in light railway development elsewhere but also has resulted in two extensions to Bank in the City and to Beckton in the Royal Docks. The 2.6km city extension to Bank was opened in July 1991. One particular aspect of civil engineering history was exposed and preserved by this excavation. The DLR extension line runs close to the Waterloo and City line, built during 1886 - 1894. The original Greathead shield used to drive that line tunnelling is still there. This has been retained in its original position, forming part of a passageway connecting the two lines. Between Tower Gate and Island Gardens Stations, the railway follows a historic west-east route through Docklands.

DLR is the cornerstone of Docklands public transport linking the City to East London at Stratford, Island Gardens and Beckton. The terminus of the line at Island Gardens on the south side of the Isle of Dogs is sited near the entrance to the Greenwich Foot Tunnel. The style of architecture for the station is said to echo the dome and curve of the Greenwich Observatory on the other side of the river. Plans are in hand for an extension from Mudchute on the Isle of Dogs under the river to Greenwich and on to Lewisham where there will be an interchange with British Rail.

HM The Queen opening DLR in July 1987

Docklands Light Railway route

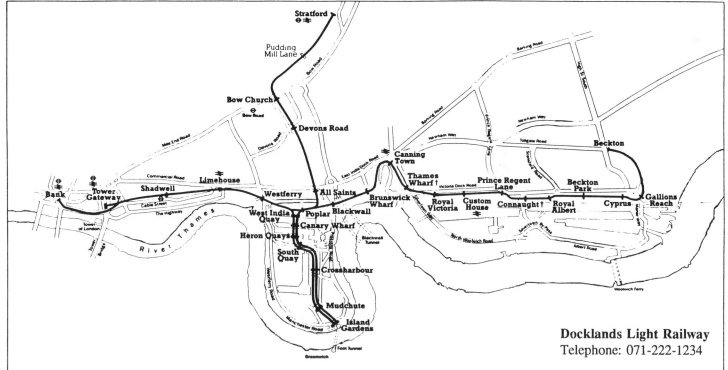

Docklands Light Railway
Telephone: 071-222-1234

128

JUBILEE TUBE LINE

The Jubilee Line Extension is a one billion pounds tube line designed to meet the expanding community and business needs of London Docklands. The 15.4km line will provide a fast transport link between Green Park, in the heart of the West End, taking a route south of the Thames via Waterloo to Canary Wharf on the Isle of Dogs and beyond to Stratford in the East. Construction began in 1991 with a projected opening date of 1996. The London Docklands Development Corporation has proposed an additional branch using the North London tracks through the Royal Docks to the existing rail terminal at North Woolwich. By providing better links between Docklands parts and residential areas south of the Thames as well as the main line stations of Waterloo, London Bridge and the City, it is a major improvement to London's transport networks. It is one of Britain's biggest Civil Engineering transport projects in the 1990's. The scheme consists of twin bore single-tracked tunnels with eleven new stations and four crossings of the Thames. The construction contracts are let in nine packages as shown in the map below.

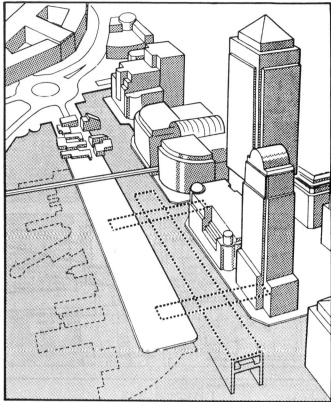
Canary Wharf Station below West India Dock

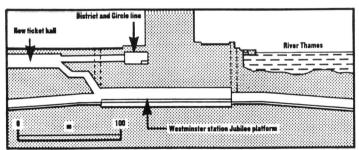
Section through proposed Westminster Station

Section through Canary Wharf Station

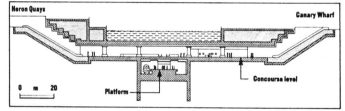

Jubilee line extension route and construction

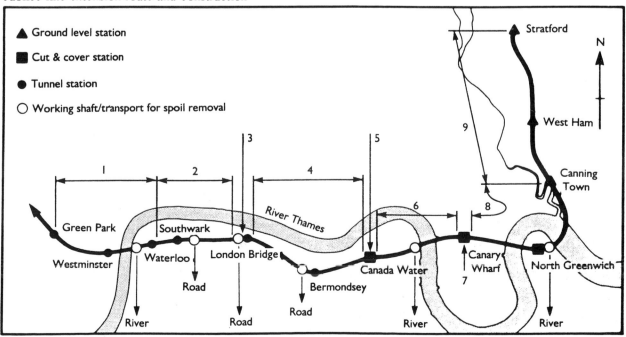

DOCKLANDS HIGHWAY

The spine of the new road network to serve Docklands north of the Thames is the Docklands Highway. This is a series of new highways and road improvement works which provide a four lane highway from the City in the west through the northern parts of the Isle of Dogs to serve Canary Wharf and other major developments across the Leamouth, through the Royal Docks to connect with the A13 at its junction with the M11/A406 North Circular link. The highway is a northern relief road running south and parallel to the A13. The central section is in place. The western section, the Limehouse Link, will be ready by 1993. The eastern section, which is vital for the development of the Royal Docks, has been opened. The various parts of the route are briefly described below.

Limehouse Link is a four lane cut and cover tunnel between Limehouse and Westferry Road. It is an artery connecting Canary Wharf and Docklands to the City and West End.

Westferry Circus is an impressive two-level roundabout designed and built by Olympia and York as part of the Canary Wharf developments.

South Poplar Link has four lanes linking Westferry Road junction with a two level Preston Road junction.

East India Dock Tunnel is a six lane section from Preston Road junction to Leamouth Road roundabout and a continuation to a new junction with the A13 just west of the Iron Bridge.

Lower Lea Crossing of four lanes cross Leamouth to a new Silvertown Way roundabout in the Royal Docks. The route continues to North Woolwich.

Connaught Crossing is a north-south across the Royal Docks with a swing bridge and feeds directly into London City Airport.

Royal Albert Dock Road is a dual carriageway along the north side of the Royal Albert Dock between Connaught Crossing and the Gallions roundabout. The Beckton extension of the Docklands Light Railway runs partly between the lanes with stations within the two main roundabouts.

Eastern Gateway Access Road has four lanes linking Gallions roundabout to the junction of the A13 and A406 roundabout and connecting via the North Circular Road to the M11.

Spurs from the Docklands Highway serve areas in the Isle of Dogs and the Royal Docks.

Map of Docklands Highway

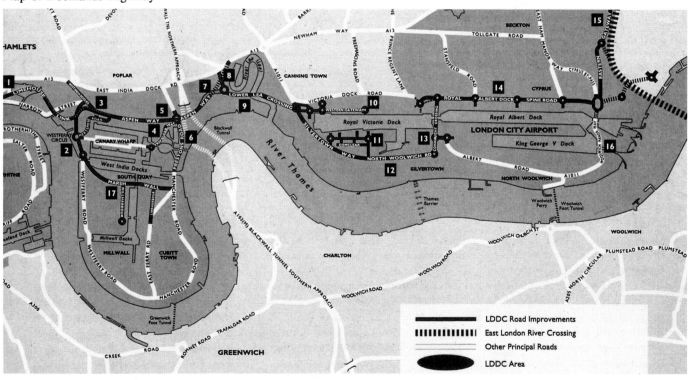

The key to new road improvements:

(1) Limehouse Link, (2) Westferry Circus, (3) Poplar Link, (4) Trafalgar Way, (5) Prestons Road Flyover, (6) Prestons Road Widening, (7) East India Dock Tunnel, (8) Leamouth Road, (9) Lower Lea Crossing, (10) Western Gateway, (11) Comclear, (12) North Woolwich Road, (13) Connaught Crossing, (14) Royal Albert Dock Spine Road, (15) Eastern Gateway Access Road, (16) Bacule Bridge, (17) Enterprise Zone Road widening

LIMEHOUSE LINK

The Limehouse Link, a 1.8 kilometre road, mostly in a cut and cover tunnel, connecting Wapping Highway to Westferry Road and the Poplar link, provides an access to Canary Wharf. The road passes under the north side of Limehouse Basin, turns south to pass under Limekiln Dock and Dundee Wharf and joins Westferry Road at a major signalling junction. The proximity of housing, the DLR and dock walls, the extensive existing road and utility system and the difficult ground conditions make the project the most complex and expensive road scheme ever constructed in the UK.

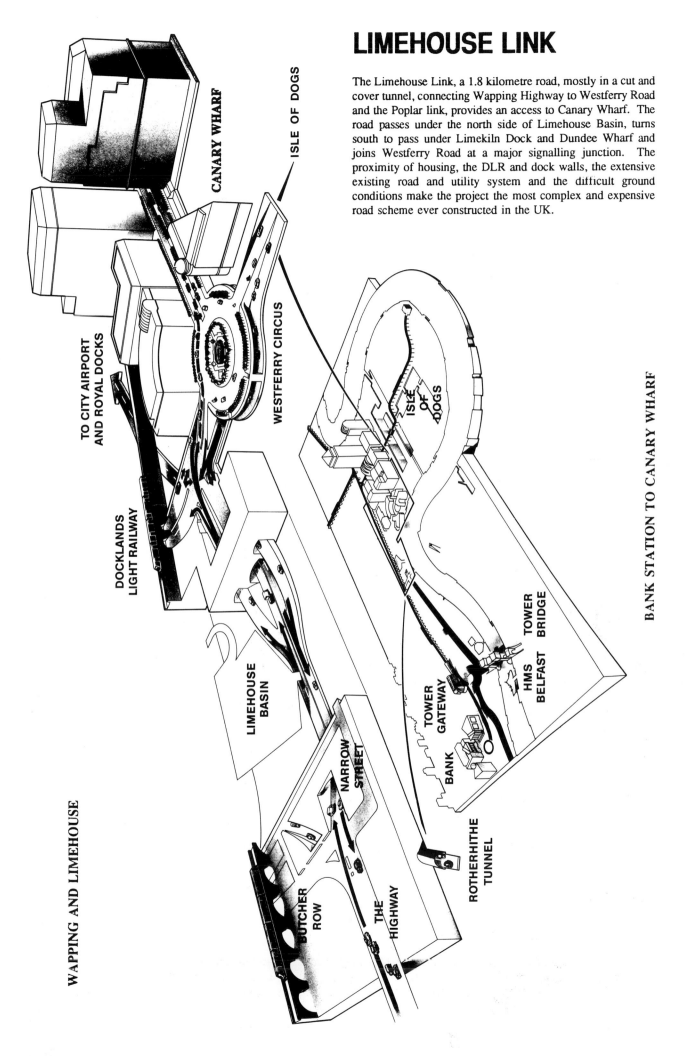

CANARY WHARF

ISLE OF DOGS

TO CITY AIRPORT AND ROYAL DOCKS

WESTFERRY CIRCUS

DOCKLANDS LIGHT RAILWAY

LIMEHOUSE BASIN

WAPPING AND LIMEHOUSE

NARROW STREET

BUTCHER ROW

THE HIGHWAY

ROTHERHITHE TUNNEL

ISLE OF DOGS

BANK STATION TO CANARY WHARF

TOWER GATEWAY

BANK

HMS BELFAST

TOWER BRIDGE

LONDON CITY AIRPORT

The Royal Docks is home to Britain's only urban airport - London City Airport. It provides regular links with UK destinations and western Europe including Paris, Brussels, Rotterdam, Lille and Strasbourg. The airport has approval to expand its destinations up to 1000 miles away which will enable it to reach cities such as Frankfurt and Rome. A quarter of a million passengers, mainly business people, are currently handled manually and it is forecast to increase to over one million by the beginning of the 21st century. The terminal building has a business centre with meeting rooms, secretarial services, as well as the upper floor bars and restaurant affording fine views of King George V Dock.

The runway has been extended by 169m eastward to a total of 1200m, it allows the operation of BAE1 Whisper jet aircrafts from April 1992 with an actual range of 900 miles (1440km) as well as a range of turbo-prop aircrafts. The destinations will include Zurich, Oslo, Stockholm, Vienna, Berlin, Milan and Madrid in addition to the present flights. [4]

London City Airport
King George V Dock, E16.
Telephone: 071-474-5555

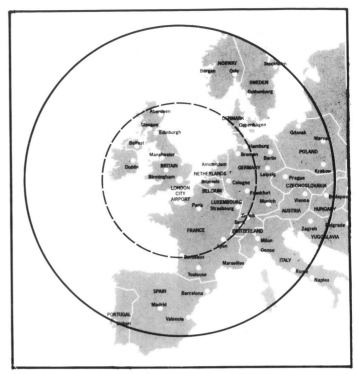

Destinations for the expanded London City Airport

London City Airport terminal

THAMES RIVERBUS

The Thames - London's oldest and broadest river highway - is part of public transport to London Docklands through the River Bus. The service includes all the piers in the west from Chelsea Harbour to the Royal Docks in the east on both the north and south banks of the river. A fleet of 62-seater catamarans runs regular and scenic services for commuters and visitors throughout the year. Canary Wharf and London City Airport (LCA) have been fully integrated in the schedule of operation with a continuous service to the airport from Charing Cross Pier every 20 minutes. Airport buses shuttle from LCA Pier to the terminal buildings in the Royal Docks. Passengers could be airborne within 50 minutes of their departure the West End.

The Riverbus Charing Cross Pier

The Riverbus catamaran

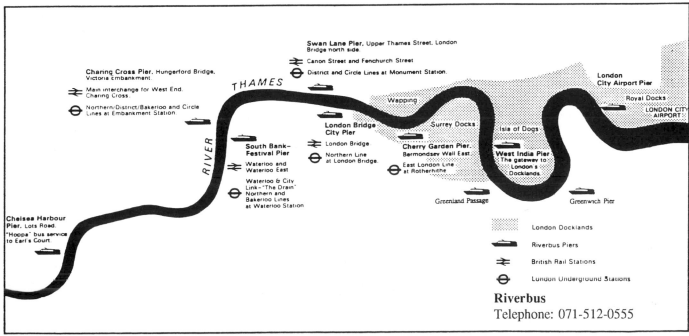

Map of the Riverbus route

INDEX

ACKNOWLEDGEMENTS

I gratefully acknowledge the debt I owe to my institution, The University of East London, for its support of the research work over many years. I am most grateful to many individuals, previous writers, and organisations who so kindly assisted with the preparation of the book.

For the supply of considerable information and for the kind permission to reproduce the photographs and illustrations, I am deeply grateful to the London Docklands Development Corporation (LDDC) and its officers. In particular I wish to record my sincere thanks to Gary Jewell for his invaluable help and co-operation. Thanks are also due to Geoff Nyberg for helpful suggestions and the supply of slides and maps, all of which are the copyright of the LDDC.

To Olympia & York special thanks are given for the supply and permission to reproduce photographs and maps of Canary Wharf including those for the book covers. I am very grateful to Tom Samson of Chorley and Handford for providing aerial photographs and useful information.

For the supply of information and help generally I am grateful to many people and organisations but special mention should be made of Docklands News, Docklands Magazine, Port of London Authority and their Magazine, New Civil Engineer, Dock and Harbour Authority and their Journal, Construction Weekly, Geonex Story Ltd, Butlers Wharf Ltd, St. Martins' Property Corporation, St. Katharine by the Tower Ltd., Jacobs Island Company, Anchor Brewhouse, Barratt East London, Broseley Estates, Costain Homes, Daniel Homes, Ideal Homes, Heron Homes, Laing Homes, Lovell Farrow Ltd, Regalian Properties, Roger Malcolm, Wates Homes, Wimpey Homes Holdings, Rosehaugh Copartnership, Conran Roache, Tobacco Dock Developments Ltd, Trafalgar House Residential, Wiggins Property Group, Colin Druce & Co, Docklands Light Railway, London City Airport, John Mowlem Ltd and Thames Line.

For assistance with the historical research, I wish to record my deepest thanks to Terry O'Connoll for his loyal support and valuable information. Photographs were kindly supplied by various shipping lines which operated in the former docks, including Ben Line, Ellerman Line, Harrison Line and Fred Olsen Line. Thanks are due to Captain G. Nicholson and Captain D J Cranna. Acknowledgement is made to the valuable assistance received from Laurence Stratford of the Daily Telegraph.

I would like to thank sincerely Joanna Maddison for her extremely valuable work in typing the whole manuscript many times, with great skill and care. Her patience, dedication and co-operation throughout the various stages of preparation of the book are greatly appreciated.

I would like to express my gratitude to Ted Weedon for many valuable suggestions and expert proof reading, Derek Merritt for his unstinting support and kind help over many years, Margaret Youngman for excellent proof reading and numerous useful suggestions, Sheila Millard for general advice, Ron McDougall for valuable discussions and useful suggestions, R Vasanthakumaran for considerable help with the preparation of maps, Alan Hooker for his constant help and advice on the operation of the wordprocessor, John Noble for preparing the excellent index, Phillip Jupp for artwork, Barry Nottage for library research and external contacts, Sheila Johnson for administration of research grants, David Hilling for helpful information and Reg Schofield for kind support and encouragement.

I also thank many other people who helped including Derek Hart, Ruth Thraves, Carole Anthony, Helen Pallett, Anne Kropholler, John Williams, Janine Grimmond, Brenda Grebol, Terry Hatton, Walter Kalakua, Jim James, Jean Merritt, Joan Mouyia, Anna Bass, Sandra Zahra, Hettie Nelson, Angus Rankine, Karen Hutchinson, Collette Fury, Kathleen Barnhill, Nicky Burston, Cliff Randall, Tony Stanton Precious, Carole Lyders, Gordon Graham, David King, N Kent, C Versey, Sheila Mead and Ray Vickers.

I am most grateful to my wife Irene, for her understanding and forbearance over many months during the compilation of the book. Thanks are due to my son Rodney, for reading the manuscript and making valuable suggestions, and also to my daughter Karen for general help. I owe a debt of gratitude to John Jones for acting as an art consultant, helpful comments on the book layout and many hours of patient discussions.

Finally, I would tender my sincere thanks to the readers of my books to whose kindly letters and encouragement the latest publication owes much.

St Katharine Docks